Stress Free Leadership

Training Secrets to Leverage Employees and Build a 7 Figure Business

Susan Delano Swim

Stress Free Leadership

ISBN-13: 978-1-7328719-0-8
ISBN-10: 1-7328719-0-6

Published by: Celebrity Expert Author
http://celebrityexpertauthor.com

Canadian Address:	US Address:
1108 - 1155 The High Street,	1300 Boblett Street
Coquitlam, BC, Canada	Unit A-218
V3B.7W4	Blaine, WA 98230
Phone: (604) 941-3041	Phone: (866) 492-6623
Fax: (604) 944-7993	Fax: (250) 493-6603

TABLE OF CONTENTS

FOREWORD

I AM OFTEN ASKED to write the foreword to business related books, and it is a pleasure for me to introduce Susan's second book for entrepreneurs. With over 30 years of helping people successfully create wealth, I know how hard it is to do without the right guidance. I understand how especially challenging it is to run a service related company with employees and turn a profit without running your business and life into the ground.

Susan knows this firsthand, as you will find out from her bathroom mirror moment when she looked herself in the eyes and decided that she was not going to let her company and staff drive her insane. I tend to be wary of most business coaches who are eager to advise you on running a business when they have never supported their livelihood through any enterprise of their own. This is not the case with Susan. She has cracked the code on how to engage employees and create a team that is dedicated to serving clients and growing the profits of the company they work for.

I have worked with people from all walks of life who want to become wealthy and break free from the shackles of a job through entrepreneurship. The business owner in a service industry with employees is a very special breed of entrepreneur. When I encounter these people, they are usually overwhelmed, beaten down and stressed out from the never-ending demands of their clients and employees. Worst of all, they are usually charging far too little, paying way too much and barely scraping by. Most of them feel that this is not what they signed up for and are looking for a way to simplify things and make a good living much more easily.

"Stress-Free Leadership--Training Secrets to Leverage Employees and Build a 7-Figure Business" reveals the exact steps that Susan took to go from working 18 hours a day and barely making ends meet, to spending time on the water, time with her daughters and grandchildren while the company runs itself. As the owner and leader of a window cleaning / caulking company, she and her husband created high-performance teams of seasonal laborers who are dedicated to the success and profitability of the company.

This sounds like a dream to most employers. It is so hard to get employees motivated to care about anyone other than themselves, let alone provide great customer service and dedication to the vision of the organization. You'll discover throughout the chapters of this leading-edge book, how you can apply simple principles to become the leader that people are inspired to follow. You will be delighted to find that it is not that hard to quickly bring employees into alignment, get them working efficiently and generating more profit per hour.

The read is quick and easy right from the beginning, where you get Susan's insights on how to hire properly to build your team. She shows you how to listen to what they are not telling you and spot traits and talents that identify a person who is worthy of investing time and money into training. You'll learn how to decide when to spend money on expensive training for skilled employees and how to use this investment to create a loyal and trustworthy team player. Her stories are of the application of the tips she shares and the bottom line results that she gets by using them to speak for themselves.

As the owner of your service related business, you owe it to yourself to become the best leader you can be so that you can fully leverage the skills and talents of your employees. This involves some introspection to find out where your own mindset blocks and limiting beliefs keep employees behaving in destructive, profit-draining patterns. In the last chapter, you will find exercises and processes that will help you identify and remove habits and behaviors that make your life difficult.

By walking yourself through the five steps laid out for creating a high-performance team, you will find the excitement that you had when you started your business getting reignited. You will start seeing opportunities to improve service, cut costs and increase profits everywhere. The end result is a collaborative team of dedicated employees, who have your back and go the distance for the company because they know that everyone wins.

It is a great honor to know Susan and the amazing work that she is doing in the world. I feel a deep respect and gratitude for her dedication to the development and growth of leaders and the people who follow them. It is my wish that her words serve you well and help you to find balance, harmony and wealth in a business that you love.

Robert G. Allen
#1 New York Times
Bestselling Author

INTRODUCTION

MY NAME IS SUSAN DELANO SWIM and at the time of writing this I was the operations manager/co-owner of Clearview Integrated Window Services in Nova Scotia. I have been running this business with my husband Tony since 2004. Our business includes window cleaning, caulking, pressure washing, high rise window replacement, finding and preventing air and water penetration and organic restoration of the exterior of buildings. We specialize in window replacement programs, applying coatings and sealants, and conducting exterior envelope evaluations on buildings. Accessing the high, difficult-to-reach rigging situations with our team of specialized rope access professionals is part of our daily operations. We are a medium sized company with staff numbers ranging from 15 to 20, depending on the time of year. Since adapting a high-performance leadership style, our company sales have doubled, we have shown great growth and is now generating a nice profit. Becoming a high-performance leader, altering how I do business and who I am in our Company, has given me the space and freedom to continue to develop our company without feeling unsurmountable, unsustainable, unforgiving stress and continual pressure. Since adopting this leadership style and methods, I no longer feel stressed, become frustrated, or have work-related anxiety. *My motto is: Be what you want to see in your employees and always come from a place of respect and kindness.*

But it hasn't always been like this.

When we first bought the Company, I experienced times when I just couldn't get out of bed in the morning, thinking, "Why bother nobody listens, the work isn't getting done on time. We're losing money. So why look for more work when nobody else seems to care? We may as well just shut down the Company."

The situation was so bad that I felt the employees were running the Company, they told me what, when, where and how. Jobs weren't getting finished. Employees left jobs incomplete and didn't seem to care. Customers were upset, I was stressed and overwhelmed and at times I just buried my head, gave up, and was emotionally exhausted!

A lot of what was happening wasn't so much what the customers' experienced. It was what I experienced! There were some dissatisfied customers, and a few could turn into many very quickly if not addressed. The biggest problem we had was the lack of respect for the Company. Money was being poured down the drain and I was lost in this emotional downhill battle.

For a job that should have taken three hours, it was taking them nine hours. We were charging the customer the three hours and having to pay out nine hours of work to the employees. Back then, that was hundreds of dollars. It was our money walking out the door and I accepted our employee's rationale, knowing in my heart it was all excuses.

This was my reality: employees were padding hours and walking all over us. It was really my fault. I was allowing it to happen. I had a fear of speaking up, I didn't want to lose the employees that we did have and be left with nobody. I'd phone them and ask, "Why aren't you at the job-site?" They would be at Tim Horton's on a coffee break. Paid 15-minute breaks always took considerably longer. Their day started at 7:30 a.m. and they would clock in at 7:00 to clean up a truck that should never have been messy in the first place. They were late arriving at job sites and didn't seem to care. I had to call the customers continuously and apologize. I felt I was not able to keep my word when speaking with our customers and that just about killed me.

Does this sound vaguely familiar to you?

It came down to, "Either we make some drastic changes, or we'll have to shut the doors. It's one or the other." I couldn't do it anymore the way it was being done. All the bad habits that came with the employees from the old Company had to be "undone." I had to make the decision to take control, because employees were given the unspoken power to run the Company.

The word that struck me at that time was VICTIM! That's what a fellow coach called me once early on in my coach training days in 1999, and I had an unexpected reaction to that word. It meant I was not standing up for myself. I was not saying what needed to be said. I was devastated to have been called a victim. I knew I had put myself in that position and it was true. That word hit me at my core, made the hair stand up on the back of my neck and pushed me into action. That one day I finally realized it, was the day I actually felt like a victim and that was it for me. How did I allow this to happen and what was I going to do about it? That's when everything changed.

Vulnerability is part of being an owner of a company, embracing uncertainty, risk and emotional exposure all of which I was acutely aware of experiencing. At my core I felt fear of failure, disappointment and regret. I was aware of feeling all of this but was in denial of what the real problem was, I was frozen. When I decided enough was enough, I had been willingly sitting on the sidelines, my vulnerabilities, my insecurities became my strengths, my driving force to be brave to have the courage to step into my much-needed leadership role to make the changes that needed to be made.

Fortunately, I turned that around, and now we have employees who are time-conscious and job-conscious. They do quality work. Now the job that would have taken three hours before is taking two hours or less and is being done professionally. They are making money for the Company while meeting quality expectations. They are looking for more work to do, so they are working smarter, not harder. The point is that our employees are doing what they are supposed to do. They feel proud of their work and we are running a profitable company.

Can you say the same?

I want to hear about you sitting in your office counting your money. I want to hear about you doing more of the things that you want to do because you know that the jobs are getting done right the first time.

I want you to describe that ideal scenario. You get in your car, you turn it on, you drive it fast, it does what it's supposed to, and you're happy. You know what is under the hood, you have taken care of it and set it up, so you have expectations to receive high performance driving from your car. I want you to talk about driving the car, and it performs the way you want it to perform.

I'd like you to be able to say, "Now that our employees have dug down and understand the how to's of our business, the details such as the times and resources required, and they understand how long a job is supposed to take, they are consistently on task or taking less time to complete projects. They are looking for more ways to get jobs for the Company, and my employees are generating more business every year. The workers know that they get rewarded for performing, so they strive to perform better all the time. Their efficiency and productivity are excellent while delivering quality work resulting in satisfied customers."

There is more. Your profits have increased year after year. You have the best company in your industry in your area. You have the time to spend with your family. You do what you want. If you don't feel like going to work, you don't. I went through all these challenges, so I speak from experience.

When I tell my story to other business owners, they say, "I can't understand how your employees take less time than you have decided a job takes. I don't know how you get employees to look for new work and to take pride in doing it really well. I don't know how to do that. How do you do that, Susan?"

It is easier than you think. You become a high-performance leader and create high-performance teams that work smarter, not harder. I don't even have to be there. I can delegate and disappear.

A few of the important benefits of becoming a high performer is the way you now effortlessly work. Following your daily regime, you are energized and more productive, so you have the time to build strong relationships with your employees and your customers. The best part is you are inspired to be more creative to grow your business beyond what you thought was possible.

After implementing high-performance leadership strategies, I actually looked forward to getting out of bed every morning because I changed how I was viewing and feeling about the Company and the Company was now operating smoothly. I made a conscious decision to use my high-performance leadership skills with my work load and with the employees to get them on the Company's side of being high performers. The employees who no longer fit where relieved of their duties, giving space for new great hires that have stayed with us for years.

The idea that changed everything that day was the word and thought of being a victim, I took ownership and stepped up. I will not consciously be a victim to anybody, "I can do this," has been my motto ever since. STEP up, show your stuff, be brave, be a high-performance leader. Show them who you are and what you can do for them and the Company! This is your company, not theirs. If they don't like it, they can leave."

I stepped up as a leader and decided there were things I had to put into place to protect the Company. The employees were not responsible for putting the Company where it was. I had allowed all of this. The realization struck me, "Holy shit, I'm the one who has allowed this. I am the one who tolerated this; they were just doing what they could get away with or what was expected of them." I wasn't being the leader I needed to be, I allowed the bar to be set so low. If I were being a great leader, none of this would have happened. Everything that happens in a company starts and stops with the leader and filters down.

So, what did I do? I adapted the high-performance leadership habits. I looked inward, I developed routines, I made changes within myself. Now my employees show up on time. They finish early or look for extra work. They only clock the hours they work, and when they're not working, they're looking for new customers. We grow year after year. We're becoming bigger and bigger because we're getting more and more contracts.

What made such a dramatic difference was the shift in my own mindset, the high-performance leadership skills I embraced and the coaching I gave my employees.

In this book, I will tell you how I morphed from a depressed and unmotivated business owner to one who now runs a profitable company with an efficient and engaged workforce.

High Performance Leadership Skills - Coaching in Our Company

- Pay attention to your employees, show you care
- Promote and empower solution-seeking strategies/decisions
- Make employees feel inspired, supported, and honored
- Creativity, breaking through performance, resilience
- High performance leadership training - set boundaries and

expectations that push and empower their strengths, so they are committed to their outcomes

- Coaching tailored for all situations at any given moment
- Enable behavioral shifts at any time so they can more easily progress to feeling positive
- Trust to be and do their best
- Support them as changing demands arise
- Praise – celebrate accomplishments / successes
- Accountability – everyone is accountable
- Company vision – setting goals so employees know what part they contribute in the Company, they are a big part of the vision
- Bring in fun and laughter

High performance leadership skills improve your leadership style, enhances team performance, and supports diversity and optimism. When you can make employees feel honored and excited to work for you, they'll want to stay around, and your company will prosper.

This book is my story, what I learned from all my experiences in evolving a business from underperforming to becoming a high-performance business. The intention of this book is to provide an overview of the experiences with real life examples and provide a framework to success. I have been a certified coach since 1999 and I have lived the **_High-Performance Leadership Training Program_**, adopting all the methods to ensure success along my journey.

High-Performance Leadership Training is the training program that I offer. This program has helped thousands of business leaders become high performance leaders in their business. This training is what will take you to the next level in your business beyond what you thought was possible, and the best part is you will feel excited and energized.

I would love to connect with you, I invite you to fill out an application to talk at www.susandelanoswim.com/application or to contact me at susan@susandelanoswim.com if you would like more information about what I offer.

I look forward to hearing from you.

"Most great people have attained their greatest success just one step beyond their greatest failure."

Napoleon Hill

Be on A Mission!

Before we move on, I'd like to mention one of the very important elements of inspiration that is part of our success *The Mission Statement*. Our mission statement defines what our business and employees stand for and guides the direction in which the Company is going:

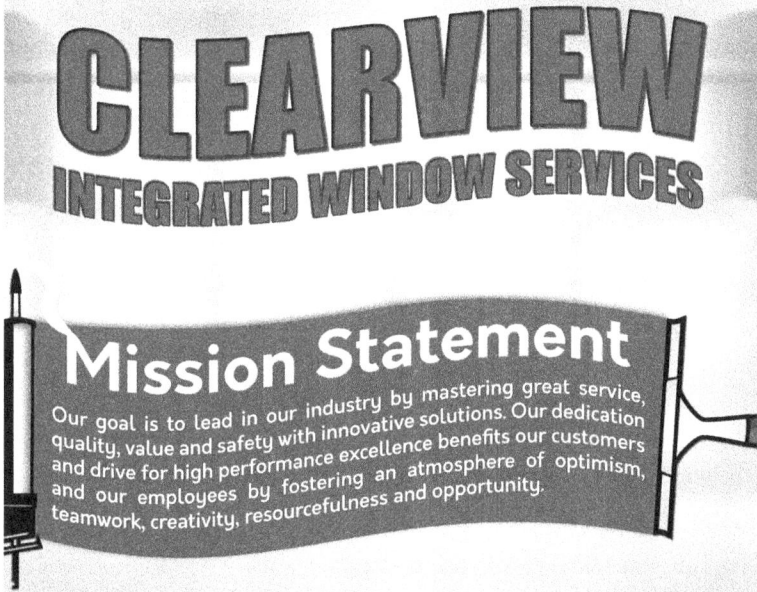

CLEARVIEW
INTEGRATED WINDOW SERVICES

Mission Statement
Our goal is to lead in our industry by mastering great service, quality, value and safety with innovative solutions. Our dedication and drive for high performance excellence benefits our customers and our employees by fostering an atmosphere of optimism, teamwork, creativity, resourcefulness and opportunity.

Why is a mission statement important for our company and for all companies?

It is our guiding light, a clear statement that states our daily intentions, our strategy for development, and the direction to which the Company is continually moving toward – our Company's purpose. Our mission statement is everything that I believe about our company, it is the way we run the business, the way we want our employees to feel about our company, and a reminder of how we work on a daily basis.

Whenever I read our mission statement, I feel its message at my core, it lifts me up and I am proud of what we have accomplished to get to this level of business. It is a reminder!

When I was creating the mission statement, I focused on three parts: what our goal was, how we serve our customers and treat our employees, and the Company's culture. When in the process of creating the mission statement, there was a certain feeling that I wanted to have. I wanted to feel proud, I wanted it to be inspiring for me and for our employees, and it had to be true to how we operate. Our mission statement inspires our teams and the leadership within the Company.

At our monthly meetings we read this statement as a team. It is empowering and reminds all of us of our path, what the Company stands for, and the direction it is headed towards. It is important for everyone to feel this.

Making the switch and embracing high performance leadership habits has made a world of difference at all levels of operation within our company and in my life. Most of the time our company is great, we are on track and climbing higher, our crews are doing exactly what they are supposed to be doing. I am not saying that everything is perfect, but I am saying that when problems arise we handle them differently, they are not such a big deal anymore. When days go off the rails, we deal and move on. This way of being and working is a huge stress relief. There used to be days when I would let our employees feel my stress which was never good. They work hard enough doing what they do, and they don't need to feel bad vibes from me.

Creating high performance leadership habits in our office has made my life 10 times easier and has dramatically increased our performance and profits. The habits and practices that I embrace every day are what has made the difference. Changing our culture and setting up the best environment and structures started at the top in our company. Once our leadership improved the environment and the culture of our company improved, new creative ideas and other valuable suggestions came in from our teams. Being open and creating this dynamic works extremely well for improvements and the evolution of the Company. Our teams see and experience things that management does not and vice versa.

My husband and I have different leadership styles. We both run our own crews and we both do what works for each crew. I am a more detail-oriented person, I ask more questions, I have my own style of figuring things out, and I expect a lot out of our teams. My husband is more relaxed, he expects a lot but also tolerates a little more than I do. When I started to operate differently, sharing high performance habits, he observed and as the time went on he started adapting the habits that worked best for him and his crew. His way works best for him and mine works best for me. If you are in a partnership, it is important that you do what is best for you and make sure you are both in alignment with your company's vision and mission. There are six high performance leadership habits, following them all is ideal and will give you the biggest impact, but even embracing a few will move you further ahead, and make you feel better in your business and in life in general. Everything that you do to better yourself in one area will naturally improve other areas and will be the stepping stone to embracing another high-performance leadership habit. High performance leadership habits are the key steps to being successful beyond what you consider to be your normal expectations of yourself and of your teams over the long term.

If you are the type of person who does not need anything or does not need help in any way, this could be an indication that means you are unconsciously closed off to continued learning and growth. That your current way of doing business is ok, that you are ok with the status quo, and you possibly think that you know everything that there is to know, and there is nothing wrong with that if it is working for you. But curiosity and self-confidence, as well as knowing there is something different that you can do is your key to success beyond what you are currently having and doing.

High Performance Leadership benefits:

- You are more successful than before embracing them
- You have less stress and cope better with stress you do have
- You are focused and don't get derailed by distractions
- You embrace challenges and enjoy them
- You are not consumed by feeling overwhelmed and anxious
- You meet and exceed your goals
- You work smarter not harder
- You become a passionate and happier force at work and at home
- You're a contagious positive influence for all those around you, they want this for themselves too
- You have a plan and you know where you are going making small adjustments along the way
- You will become more successful, making more money and having fun
- You feel empowered, you feel you are on track to greatness everyday and you know where you are going
- Life is exciting, and you are now doing everything that you knew you needed to do to be the successful leader that you knew you could be
- Sleep becomes a priority and you make sure you are well rested

Above are all the reasons why we become entrepreneurs. Starting your own business is the easy part, making it a thriving happy successful business is the work. Evolving my thinking and implementing the six high performance leadership habits has changed my world. They have made me better at what I do. I know how to reach the next level, I know what it takes to get there. It feels natural and exciting to be consistently and effectively engaging the teams and out performing myself. I went from dreading my days to being confident and experiencing joy in a very short period.

Challenging myself to be and do better, strategic planning, empowering our teams and engaging inspiration are what made the difference.

"If you are working on something exciting that you really care about, you don't have to be pushed. The vision pulls you."
Steve Jobs

Chapter 1:
CHOOSING THE RIGHT EMPLOYEE

THERE IS ONE THING that the window cleaners and caulkers like about their job: They can go anywhere in the world and get a job as long as they have the right skill set and training.

Your business, like ours, calls for specific skill sets, and the selection starts during the hiring process. I've noticed that most candidates don't have the actual skill we're looking for, but they do show ambition, energy, commitment, and the willingness to learn (we do provide training). I ask questions to find out if they have been on a team before, if they work well with other team members and with management, and if they can take directions and follow through. One of our critical skills is good customer service through listening and verbal communication as well as development and delivery of proactive solutions. Common sense is also extremely important to have and use, along with the ability to think strategically about jobs and to know the right process and the right order to get things done.

Of course, common sense is not always common practice, and it is crucial to evaluate how the candidate fares on that front.

I assess this quality (or the lack of it) through questions about their previous jobs and how they handled various situations. I create a scenario that would be common in my business and ask them for their first response. Then I ask them to get creative about how they would manage or solve it. The answer I get gives me an idea of how they would handle something that is familiar or something that is not familiar, and what their learning curve is. Being able to think outside the box makes a big difference, because it shows that the candidate is resourceful and is thinking strategically.

This is the kind of person I am looking for:

- Ambitious
- Energetic
- Loyal
- Honest
- Flexible
- Creative
- Positive
- Solution oriented
- Open and willing
- Willing to try something new and not afraid to fail
- Willing to be trained and able to handle difficult tasks
- Gets along well with other team members
- Follows directions

Reference checks will help you assess these attributes as you may not be able to through an interview.

Of course, it is possible that the candidates are just telling you what you want to hear, and I learned to discern fact from fiction. For instance, a know-it-all who says he can do everything rather than admit his limitations and the need for training, shows me the candidate is not being totally truthful.

On the other hand, someone who asks a lot of questions and says he has never done this particular work but is willing to learn and be part of the team is a good prospect. This kind of person is attractive if you are looking for a long-term employee, one to grow with the Company. But if I need a temporary or short-term worker to get us over the hump, my criteria is more focused on the skill level and getting the job done well.

In my particular industry, jobs are physically demanding so strength and endurance are essential. I can assess physical ability, agility and dexterity by the way people move. In my company having experience lifting and balancing is important, if they don't have that experience, I want to make sure they are trained properly so they don't get hurt.

During the interview process, I always ask if the candidate has any old injuries. In most cases, people are honest about this, but if someone is not truthful, then we're going to find out pretty quickly when they start working. We have a 3-month probation period and that is long enough for us to assess their ability and performance.

People who are trying to tell you what you want to hear, rather than thinking on their feet, have a way about them. The interviewee can appear to be aloof, sly, or defensive. In contrast, an interviewee who asks questions and is willing to say, "I have never done that, but I am here to learn and be part of a team," is a good candidate. A potential employee who is a know-it-all but isn't willing to learn because he thinks he knows everything will not work out in the long term.

Another very important attribute we are looking for is the ability to communicate. We can see this during the interview by how well they listen to what I am asking and how they respond. You can tell how much they're engaged in the conversation by how they're answering the questions.

This is how you evaluate the kind of employees that you're seeking in your industry. When people have businesses that provide service, there will be some similarities in the type of employees they're looking for, but there are some industry-specific abilities as well.

This is how I evaluate prospective employees:

- I ask questions about what they enjoyed and disliked about their past jobs and why they left
- I pay attention to their body language and energy
- I take note of whether they are a "yes" person
- Are they willing to learn new skills
- I ask what team sports they play or groups they belong to now or in the past. Where they leaders of these groups and/or good team players. What was their team experience?
- I notice if they are interested in learning about our company or just want to know how much they are paid and what the hours are, implying that they just want a job!
- I see what past training or certificates they are bringing with them and their interest to find permanent work in that field

When I'm hiring somebody, I want to know that these people will build on the Company's strength and that they're going to be a really good fit all the way around, with the team they're working with, and also with the Company culture. I'm looking at what their values and interests are, and how passionate they are about the work they do. If they're eager to learn and to put in the necessary effort, those are the people I want.

Whenever I'm recruiting, I'm always looking for long-term workers, unless it's a temporary contract, but I don't typically hire short-term. I want employees who will help the Company grow and bring in all the attributes I mentioned before.

I also make sure I ask questions. "What are your long-term plans? Are you interested in future trainings or travelling? Where do you see yourself in one to five years? What is your dream for your future? What skills do you bring with you?"

I will quickly find out if they are looking for a temporary job until their actual trained skill set opens up or if they are looking for permanent work. It doesn't mean I won't hire them. It's just so I know if they are a short-term or long-term employee, so how much do I want to invest in them depending on what their plans are and why the Company is hiring them.

Filling in someone's time until they get their dream job is expensive. Ask questions about their past and current trainings and if they have plans to use those trainings.

Usually, people are more than happy to show you previous trainings or certificates. Recent ones signal they're invested in that field.

Another opportunity is to get them to describe some of their previous positions. Do they talk about those optimistically, or has each of their past jobs been a problem because of the boss or co-workers? Use caution if the candidates mention problems they've had with past employers. If they bring stories of being bullied or treated unfairly and they have that similar story for more than one employer, it may be that person's theme in life.

The risk is that you'll be the next on their hit list. People who talk like that usually think they're justified, that everything that's happened to them has been bad and that they have become the victim of many situations. They usually wear that stuff on their sleeve and want to talk about it but take no responsibility for the part they played in that situation.

To assist with furthering your understanding of this, reference checks can be useful to acquire additional information from another perspective.

Always keep in mind:

- Look for personality traits. Are they willing to disagree and express why their way is better, are they willing to see their way is not better? Are they negotiable?

- Will they work independently and know they are part of a team?

- How high are they aiming for their future, do they want growth and challenges, or do they want to stay where they are, do they like the status-quo? Do they just want to survive?

- Are they personable? Will their personality fit the position? Will they fit your company culture?

- Are they positive and eager to learn?

- Are they approachable?

- Do they laugh, do they smile?

- Do they listen?

In my experience, people who may not be "fully cooked" skill-wise but have the right attitude make the best employees. The opposite, a great skillset but a rotten attitude never works out in the end. There are some businesses and roles where you must possess the basic skills because it is too time consuming and expensive to train them for this position. I would be patient to find the personality with the right attitude that fits the Company environment.

It is a bonus if someone has been working out of province in our trade, and they've decided they want to move here. They usually end up being great employees, but if we're hiring local trying to fill our team, we typically hire new people to our trade. I believe in advancement within the Company, employees in the beginning stage can go to the next level of growth in our company.

Their attitude towards the work is what I look for. For me, deciding points include their attitude towards teamwork and whether they're optimistic. If someone appears to be negative and unable to see the light in things, or they have been a victim with past employers, they will not join our team.

Our new hires come with a good attitude and have the physical ability to do the job (an important asset in our industry) but don't necessarily possess all the needed technical skills. We have an assessment program in which our supervisors and managers decide where new employees would fit best and continually assess their advancement potential.

If they start at the beginner's level, we train them not only in skills, but also with our provincial safety regulations that are in alignment with our policies and procedures, so neither they nor their teammates come to any harm while on the job.

Attitude Matters

I'm often asked whether I prefer hiring for attitude and train for skills, or hire for skills and then train for attitude?

In my experience, the first option is much better. Skills can be learned, but attitude is very difficult to change.

We once hired a person who we knew had a negative edge. He was very smart and we saw great potential but we also questioned his ability to control his emotions. After a few discussions making him aware of our concerns he understood and agreed to manage his negative thoughts. We thought/hoped with awareness and coaching he would be able to manage and not spread his negativity throughout our company. It turned out to be a terrible mistake; everyone was affected by his "bad vibes" because in the end he was *unwilling* to manage himself. If I had listened to my gut feelings, I would have never subjected myself, my partner, my employees, and the Company to this traumatic experience that had impacted the attitude and the synergy of the entire work-force, he affected our company culture. It is so important to do what you know is best and to listen/pay attention to your gut feelings. Your intuition, your gut feelings know best and are wiser than your rationalized thoughts. We have always, (except that one time) hired people with a great attitude, that felt like a great fit and trained them.

Now, if I need to hire somebody more technical, with com-puter, accounting, or similar skills, then I have to focus on their ability, and possibly do a broader search for the person with a pleasant personality as well. In fact, attitude is crucial for me. It makes all the difference between a good day and a bad day, the overall mood in the workplace, the quality of performance and productivity, as well as customer satisfaction. Your employee's attitudes will make or break you and potentially your company.

When I'm going through the interviewing process, I think it is very important to ask open-ended questions as opposed to leading ones. I've heard interviewers tell prospective employees things like "we are this type of company and we really want to see this type of attitude in our company." Naturally, the person who's being interviewed is agreeing, saying, "That's exactly who I am."

But if you ask only open-ended questions such as, "How do you see a profitable company running?" or "How do you see yourself fitting into our company?" or "Give me an example of how you were a good team player?" or "Tell me about some great work experiences that you have had? "or "Tell me about some of the worst work experiences that you have had?" or "What did you find hard about your past jobs?", these types of questions will provide good information about their attitude and expectations. This approach is important right from the beginning of the inter-viewing process.

The Cost of New Employees

Employees are the face of your company. When you hire a great employee, who is passionate and inspiring, everybody around that person can feel that energy. They want to be around that person, their energy becomes contagious.

But when you bring in an employee who is negative, edgy or has nothing good to say, people pull back. If you don't remove that person, you might lose great employees because they don't want to work in that environment. Losing a good employee over something that could have been fixed costs the company thousands and thousands of dollars.

Hiring the right person is important because it minimizes the turnover, the revolving door of people coming and going, which costs the Company a tremendous amount of money and time and it is hard on your current teams dealing with the pitfalls of having to continually train newbies.

Training the new hire is also not cheap. When you're training an employee, the whole team goes through the process of teaching the ropes to the new person, understanding each other's strengths, and how to work as a team together. While this is happening, work slows down, and profits drop.

That's why hiring the right person the first time around is going to save you money. It will also make you money because there will be less disruptions to the work flow and morale.

It's difficult to put a precise number on the cost of hiring a new employee, but I estimated the price for the whole process, including training, at $60,000 minimally. It takes us a bare minimum of six month to 2 years to train someone fully to be up to speed. In our industry, it's not just learning to do the trade and then do it well and efficiently, it is learning how they will access the area, either driving equipment, or building staging or working on the exterior envelope of sky scrapers. They must have the know-how, the confidence, and the physical ability to complete their jobs. Their trade is just one of the many aspects of their work.

If you take all of the above elements into account, it is clear why an employer wants to engage the right person from the get-go, rather than have to hire and train several times for the same position.

When I interview potential employees, I not only ask them questions but also make sure they know what kind of company I run, so that they can decide whether it's a good fit.

It's important for them to know how we do things, and what kind of people and teams they'd be working with.

However, despite all the due diligence during the hiring process, it can happen that the employee is not working out and has to be dismissed. Many employers are afraid of firing and will keep the "bad" workers far too long. I have allowed this. I have kept an employee longer than we should have, he was causing trouble and did not fit with our company anymore. This is one place I have to manage my thoughts. If I think keeping the bad employee is better than having a vacancy, I am ignoring that this employee is creating a bad situation within our company. If I go here, my priorities are lost. It is easy to get lost worrying about how you are going to complete jobs justifying why you should keep an employee that now has a bad attitude. Your great employees see and feel this as well; you will actually hear your employees say they can do anything because no one gets fired. If you do not deal with the problem person, the company as a whole is affected, it will bring everyone's attitude down if you don't put all your great people first. If you remove yourself from the emotional roller coaster of the situation and remember that your priorities are to have happy employees with a good attitude, the decision becomes very clear and easy.

There are some signs the employer should not ignore so that he or she knows when it's time to fire a worker.

Usually, there's an attitude switch, less communication with management and the team, less effort, constant complaining, justifying problems, jealousy of co-workers, becoming a snitch, complaints by co-workers and possibly customers, all of which points to the fact that their heart just isn't in their job anymore. And if their commitment level and the interest decline, it's time for them to move on before they pull the whole team down and start affecting your customers. This is something that does not happen overnight, we will make every effort to understand the problem, look for a mutual satisfying solution and if that is not possible then removal of the employee in a timely fashion is inevitable.

Be a Great Employer - Lead by Example!

I talked about what I look for and how I evaluate prospective employees, but it's as important to be aware of your own role as an employer, how can you attract the best possible talent. Here's what I found to be valuable:

Ask Yourself:

1. What is your reputation as an employer?
2. What is the message you are sending out to the world to find employees?
3. How do you feel about your company and what do you say about your company?
4. Are you proud of your company or do you feel bad, have you become negative, or could you do better?
5. How do you feel about hiring new employees: do you dread

the process or are you willing to put in the time needed to find the right person?

6. Are you hiring the first person who walks in because you feel there is no one else out there who is a better candidate?

7. How do you feel about your employees? Do you call them names, i.e.: idiots, behind their backs?

My experience has shown that there are a lot of great prospects out there. If you find that you are only attracting the "wrong" people, it may be because you don't have the right attitude going into the process, you are not asking the right questions or you're not recruiting in the right market. Perhaps you are not thinking positively about your company or about your hiring process, those thoughts will filter down to the type of prospective employees you are searching for. I was in a conference not long ago and heard a business owner refer to all of his employees as "idiots". He was looking to find faithful hard workers but didn't show that he valued any of the current employees that he had including the ones that came to that conference with him. You get what you think, if all you are thinking is "they are idiots" that is what you will attract, that is how you will treat them and how they will treat you. No wonder they are not faithful long-term employees. If you are thinking faithful hardworking great employees your mind shifts to see them differently, to see them as great employees and then you will treat them and value them that way. You do get what you think!

You, as the employer, set up the mood, the dynamics and the culture of the Company. Your leadership is everything. The bottom line is that if you want great employees, you must be a great employer. Our leadership leads the way, we create an environment that is friendly, supportive and respectful. We treat everyone with the respect, kindness and professionalism that we expect in return, we lead the way!

Creating employee engagement and loyalty is a big part of my company culture. I always:

- Share my vision for the Company, goals and plans
- Encourage growth and advancement, make promotion path public knowledge
- Share my expertise but don't micromanage
- Suggest improvements
- If conflict is present always deal with it immediately head on
- Trust employees to do their best
- Show appreciation
- Pay attention to employee and team morale, provide support
- Empower employees to make decisions, be responsible and accountable
- Encourage creativity and new ideas
- Allow them to own up to mistakes and move forward
- Give feedback in a positive way
- Acknowledge good work and celebrate successes
- Leverage their strengths
- Remove toxic employees before they "poison" the whole workplace
- Go above and beyond the call of duty so they feel fulfilled
- Do what I say I am going to do
- 100 % of the time come from a place of kindness
- Show respect

In return, I have happy employees who show up on time, are eager and excited, and know what they need to do. They're team players. I trust my employees to do the job to the best of their ability and to represent the Company and themselves in a way that would make management and employees proud. We have their back and support them in every way that we can, so that they can thrive, and they know I will never throw them under the bus.

Of course, not everyone is a natural leader. Fortunately, positive high-performance leadership skills can be developed through training / coaching / mentoring. The first step is to change your perspective, the way you look at things, especially if you tend to focus on the negative side of your business and your employees which is easy to do, and it is contagious. From experience, I know that working your "positivity muscle" will help. What exactly does this method entail?

Here are seven steps to engaging your positivity muscle to become a positive leader:

1. Create a clear picture of what you want to achieve and how you will go about it today. What steps can you take to improve your leadership skills today? (Remember: Your beliefs are your power engine, so empower yourself to have positive inspiring thoughts, think outside the box). Bring your business dream to fruition, set an action plan from here.

2. What does your life and your business look like, say, a year from now, when the Company is working well and is profitable? Take a minute and visualize this then start to build a vision board that tells your future story.

3. Every morning focus on all the good things that are in your life, include both your personal and professional worlds. Show gratitude and appreciation at the start of each day to all your employees and for your business. Focusing only on your problems is a tough way to start your day and your employee's day.

4. Spend 80 percent of your time concentrating on the positive great aspects of your company, and the other 20 percent on finding solutions to whatever doesn't work or needs improving. When you concentrate on the positive aspects of your business, solution seeking becomes a lot less stressful and is part of your growth.

5. Office Awareness: Stop and check in with your thoughts before you enter your office, make sure you are in the right frame of mind to run your business. Let go of all personal drama so it does not consume your thoughts for the day. Start your day with an inspirational mantra that makes you feel empowered and positive.

6. Project Positive Energy: Find the good in all situations and people around you, even those that are negative or angry. In your mind see others by projecting positive messages, ie: "I wish the best for you", or "I wish you well".

7. When you first sit at your desk, fill out your daily planner sheet to set up your day up with a productive plan to get done all that is important. Write down the three best things you must do to make money that day or to move your business forward. There is a daily planning sample sheet at the end of the book or you can download the daily planner sheet at www.susandelanoswim.com/daily

"We generate fears while we sit, we overcome them by action."

Dr. Henry Link

Start every day with these basic daily "check-ins", go over the above points so they become a routine habit that will naturally and seamlessly start your day on the right side.

Bonus Tip: Set daily intentions, your intention is how you want to experience your day, the experience you can achieve regardless of the outcome. This is how you want to be doing what you do no matter what is happening.

Becoming a high-performance leader is stepping into self-mastery. Every single moment of every single day you can control your focus and your intentions. The key to self-confidence is being consistent, being aware and being honest with yourself that you are doing all that you can do. Implementing new daily practices that feel good are the beginning of this new journey. You are the creator of your own reality so be aware of the reality that you are creating and always do what feels great.

"The only limit to our realization of tomorrow will be our doubts of today."
                                    Franklin D. Roosevelt

You have great skills and ambition and you've learned plenty by having your business get you to where you are today. Your employees stay long term and they are all team players, but you didn't always have that. Even when you think you have a great team of people, things can shift with one person deciding they want something different, no matter how great you treat them. When it's time for them to move on, it is time for them to move on and trust that someone great will show up sooner than you think.

Many businesses decide, "Oh, we need someone," so they post an ad and then see what's coming in the door, but you must have processes and procedures. When I'm looking for an employee, I want to ensure that, they know what I'm asking them to join. They must know what kind of company they're joining and the team they'd be working with. Let them know what is in it for them.

In this chapter, we discussed the process of hiring great employees, looking for the right kind of person, and the importance of a great attitude. We also discussed the expense of hiring new employees, leading by example, and how to ensure that you are a great employer as well.

Here's a quick summary of the main points:

- Attitude is everything
- Importance of hiring the right employee
- The kind of employee we look for - 13 attributes
- Asking great questions to get to know why an employee wants to work for you
- How to evaluate potential employees
- Importance of attitude
- Cost of hiring new employees
- Being a great employer, leading by example
- Questions for self-reflection
- Company culture
- Steps to improve your positivity muscle

Being an entrepreneur is exciting; it encompasses your passion and your desires. But it is hard work, long hours, and it comes with many different demands and rewards. One of the biggest is managing your leadership style, for yourself and your teams. As the owner, you are '**ON**' 100 % of the time. You are being watched for everything that you say, that you don't say, how you say it, how you don't say it, what tone you use, what expression you use, how your employees feel when you talk to them, what they don't feel (for instance, appreciated), if you look at them or away from them. I frequently hear assumptions that employees make about their employers, which are not favorable. Every one of your actions or non-actions is observed, how proactive you are as a leader, and the possibility of being viewed as a boss that favors other employees, it is never ending when dealing with different personalities. Employees don't miss a beat and everything that happens points to you. Your company culture defines how you want it to be and the message you send out will result in the way your employees view you and your company. This message is in direct correlation to how they perform, whether or not they respect you and what is tolerated.

The single most important factor in any business is the leadership style that you bring into your company. What you do and what you don't do. Your leadership style is everything to the success or lack of success you experience. Your actions and your words must be in alignment. A leader must do what they say they are going to do, if you don't, your employees will not trust you or believe that you will do what you say you will do. If this is to happen, you are on a very slippery slope with your employees.

Don't make your employees guess, make sure they know everything about you, your style, your expectations and the Company that they need to know to thrive. Make this simple for your employees; this will make your life as the leader simpler too.

" Do what you can with all you have, wherever you are."
Theodore Roosevelt

In Chapter 2, we'll discuss another important topic: How to create policies that empower your employees to make good decisions.

Chapter 2:
BEING A GOOD BOSS

WE TALKED ABOUT EVERYTHING that's involved in finding and hiring good people for your company, and one of the elements I mentioned was the importance of being a good employer, the kind who attracts and retains employees.

It's important that employees feel like there's something at your company for them, more than a job. It is important that they understand that you are paying attention to them and that their contributions are making a positive difference. It is important for them to know if they want their position to change, grow, and evolve, they are encouraged to develop a plan to do that.

I admit that I did not always have this awareness. It came with experience and being open to adopting change. At the very beginning, I wasn't as conscious about creating a company culture that fostered and encouraged empowerment and opportunities for our teams. I wasn't conscious of the company culture that just happened and how bad it was. I was in survival mode and just wanted our crews to do their jobs. I wasn't happy dreading every day, looking straight into the problems, stressing out and not sleeping. At one point, I was feeling like it would be better to just close the Company and go get an hourly paid job. My focus was not on growth or culture, it was on survival. Just surviving, barely getting through every day is not a good business plan, it is anything but. This is where a lot of business owners are.

In time, I realized that either I had to step up as an owner and leader, to develop and grow the Company the way I had dreamt it would be (happy with inspired goal-oriented employees) with more flow and ease for me, or I was going to stay in this cranky position where things weren't going well.

There was one moment, I was looking in the mirror and I finally asked myself, "What are you doing? You need to step up as a leader because your employees are only behaving and acting the way you are allowing them to. If you don't change how you see your company and what you expect from yourself and from your employees, then this is what you're going to get."

From that moment on, I knew I had to change everything: what I expected from myself, my employees, what I tolerated, and what kind of leadership I provided. I had to shake up how I viewed the future of the business, I had to find my passion for it and get creative specializing in niches that allowed us to become the "go-to" Company.

The learning curve was steep, but I was able to see myself and the business in a different light and turn our company around. When I stopped hovering over the problems and saw the potential, a thousand pounds was lifted off my shoulders. The Company became exciting and I was excited by its potential.

I have been a coach since 1999 and I have used every skill in my coaching leadership tool box in this company working with our employees, my partner and our customers. Having all these skills is one thing and then using them is another, it has been a huge asset. Removing myself from the daily emotional bump and grind and stepping into a strong leadership role bringing forth all my leadership practices is what made the difference.

I genuinely care about and respect our employees. I value and appreciate their input, and I tell them that. I show my gratitude in many ways. For example, I will pop by job sites and give them gift cards for coffee, lunch, or another treat. I tell them they're doing a great job and how happy we are with their work and dedication as well as having them as part of our team.

Of course, your appreciation should be expressed not just with words, but with actions too. The best way to achieve this is to create an environment where employees have opportunities to fulfil their potential.

Let's start with…

Empowering Employees to Make Good Decisions

A big part of how I operate is I pay attention, listen, and encourage employees to bring me their ideas on how the Company can improve to make their job easier, more efficient, and to make the customers happier, so that the Company and employees can make more money. Every time you make an improvement, it affects your bottom line one way or the other. I'm always willing to look at and try anything that affects the bottom line in a positive light.

In my experience, one way of creating employee loyalty and engagement is to make them feel that they are an integral part of the Company, that their work matters, is valued and appreciated. Implementing their ideas for improvements is one way you can prove their engagement is important and valuable and that in turn builds employee loyalty.

A big part of this mindset is encouraging employees to have a say in what changes and improvements could be made so their job is easier, more efficient and, of course, more profitable for all of us. This kind of all-inclusive approach is good for the employees, but also for the Company. In other words, everybody wins.

As I mentioned before, I welcome employee input concerning any improvements they think should be made in the workplace, and I actively encourage them to participate in the decision-making process. We have different policies and procedures in place for our supervisors, team leads and team members as to what they can do and what we want them to do. It gives them the guidelines on how far they can go, and in case of uncertainly, they know who to call for guidance and support.

This is what I do to encourage employees to make decisions:

1. I create clear policies and make sure employees know the Company protocol

2. I ask for ideas and input, I validate if it will work and always provide explanations. I never just listen and do nothing about it, as lack of feedback will make employees feel ignored and they might adopt the attitude of "why bother"

3. By listening, responding, and expressing my appreciation, communication makes employees feel valuable and important

4. I encourage participation through suggestions, and "trial and error" approach, mistakes mean we are encouraging growth

5. I have a legacy of command, make sure employees know where to make suggestions or where to go if they have problems

6. I don't push employees into jobs that they're not comfortable with, but if they naturally gravitate toward them, we provide access to the training, so they can succeed

7. Give credit to employees for the Company improvements and share with the whole team

I find that when employees know that I give them leeway and trust them to make the right choices, they feel empowered and they never take advantage of this freedom. Because we have guidelines in place, they know how far they can go.

Allowing employees to make decisions is particularly critical when they are working on a job site. A customer may want some extra work done and employees know that they have the freedom to complete or refer this additional service without having to call the office.

Having guidelines and procedures in place takes away all the stress of guessing or having to get approval from management. It gives employees confidence in their ability to make decisions on behalf of the Company.

I want to emphasize one point that I made above: the chain of command and why I find it so important. It means all teams have a go-to person in case of questions or problems. Everyone in the Company knows who their "go-to" person is. Typically, only a phone call is needed to get answers. I don't want our employees running off a job site when a phone call would do. If the job requires assistance from a different expert, then we arrange it. We have various people in our company with skills in different areas who will step in when needed. The important thing to know is who to contact with a particular query.

Once an employee called me about a problem he had with his supervisor. I asked him if he followed the protocol by talking with the other person involved, to discuss his concerns. What is important here, is that under our chain of command, an employee first talks with the person involved. If that doesn't work out, he goes to his supervisor, and if that doesn't work, then he takes the issue to management. This particular employee was a little nervous about going to the person because he was also his supervisor. Once he was reminded of our company protocol and the correct person to speak with, it turned out well but if he had not followed it and had gone in a roundabout way and had not followed protocol, it would have become a different story. Our employee was grateful that he was able to handle the situation directly and all was solved.

This leads me to the next crucial factor in creating a culture of employee empowerment and decision-making.

The Importance of Communication

High-performance leadership teams start with clear and open communication. Each of the seven points outlined are about communication proving that communication is the cornerstone of employee engagement and of successful organizations. Everything listed: Informing employees about the Company policies, procedures, chain of command, encouraging ideas and suggestions, and expressing appreciation for their work is a form of communication.

Communicating is a huge part of a successfully run company. How do you communicate; Phone, text, in person? How do you convey who is the best person to have on certain job sites or solve personnel problems? We have policies around the credentials required to do particular jobs. Is your communication clear so that your teams know exactly who is doing what so there is no confusion?

I prefer person-to-person interaction, where I can see the person's face and read their body language. I like to hear the emotion in their voice; tension or anticipation. I pay attention to other non-verbal signs. I listen and pay attention to their breath as well. If someone's holding their breath or they are barely breathing or taking short quick breaths, there might be something going on that you should questioned. I pay attention to all aspects of our interactions to make sure nothing is missed. I want to make sure if an employee comes to me, nothing is overlooked.

If I suspect there's something they're not telling me, I will provide the space and time during our conversation to allow our employees to feel comfortable to express what needs to be said. Very often, they take my lead and say something like, "Well, actually this happened, and it freaked me out." We are on construction sites a lot, so maybe there was a close call on a site that almost hurt somebody or hurt them. If that's the case, we come up with preventative solutions to protect everyone.

Of course, sometimes in-person communication is not possible.

Texting does have its place for certain things, especially if you need to get a message to your staff quickly and they're working with a client and it would be inappropriate to be talking on the phone, it works for certain situations. I can't always be in front of our employees, so it does serve a purpose, but texting is not an effective way to discuss problems. Texting can be misinterpreted even with the best of intentions and should never be the means of conversation or replace "one on one" conversations with employees. At the end of the day and for all situations and circumstances, employees know I'm there for them no matter what it is.

Causes of communication breakdown:

1. **Inattentiveness** – not paying attention
2. **Disorganized organization** – indecisive leadership, time pressures, no set teams
3. **Conversations** – lack of intentions, not dealing with the issues, not being direct
4. **Incongruent** – Leadership says one thing and does another
5. **Negativity** – nothing good to say

Poor communication leads to low employee morale and productivity. There are many fall outs that can happen when the communication either doesn't exist or is broken:

1. Your employees will feel you don't care so why should they
2. They are less engaged and don't feel empowered
3. They become frustrated

4. They don't know where or if they belong

5. They don't understand the Company vision, or that they are an integral part of it

6. They loose respect for their leaders and the Company

7. Negative talk starts amongst the employees, conflicts fester

Great communication

1. **Prior to the conversation, set your intention** – Setting your intention is the experience you want to achieve regardless of the outcome for this meeting. Know the best desired outcome and set the intention for who you want to be during the meeting. For example; my intentions: I, the boss want to be kind, honest and brave, to listen and say what needs to be said always coming from a place of kindness. Conversation outcome: The best possible outcome would be to continue working with this great employee

2. **Social Media** – Turn off all bells and whistles before the meeting starts it shows you are paying attention and that they are important

3. **Listening** – Give the conversation space, don't jump in, let them express themselves so everything gets said and nothing is missed

4. **Repeat what you heard for clarification;** "This is what I heard, is that what you meant?"

5. **Be Present** – Look at the person you are with (make eye contact), be attentive and show you care

6. **Be Congruent** – Do what you say you are going to do and do it in the time frames agreed upon

7. **Be positive**

8. **Follow up** – Always check in to see if things are improving or if adjustments need to be made.

When you have great communication in your company your employees know where they belong. Communication increases their morale and productivity as they know exactly what they are supposed to be doing, who they are working with and what the best end result is. They are part of the inspired team leading the vision of the Company and they don't have to second guess anything or anyone. Good communication is one of the leading skills to running a successful company.

"Don't work for recognition but do work worthy of recognition."

H. Jackson Brown, Jr.

To Err is Human

Of course, when you empower employees to make decisions, mistakes are bound to happen.

Unintentional mistakes are part of growth, I am not going to react in a negative way. There is a trial and error period when trying something for the first time. My attitude is that screw-ups can happen to all of us. We look to see and understand what went wrong, why it happened and focus on finding solutions.

You can't expect your teams to experiment and grow if you're going to penalize them for mistakes. That is not how I build employee engagement and loyalty. My way of handling mistakes is to tell employees, "Let's figure out why this happened, and let's find a solution so it doesn't happen again."

When employees feel that you're looking out for them, they start to look out for you too. It creates an unspoken bond of trust and mutual respect. They know that they can come to me with anything, admit mistakes or mishaps that happened, and I'm not going to be upset or be angry. They know that I respect them for coming to me. In my world, there is no room for outrage, anger or walking away from an employee with a problem, only respect, kindness and solution seeking.

As I said, I always encourage ideas on how to improve any aspect of the job, and when mistakes occur, what is the best way to resolve them. Employees know that I listen to every suggestion and if it turns out to be a good one, it will (after we test it to see whether it works well for us) become a procedure/ policy within the Company. This approach makes employees feel that their contributions are important to the whole organization, and that their input is valued.

This is great for the Company because when employees are happy, productivity goes up, cost and waste go down, team collaboration is in sync, and customers are satisfied. It's a win-win situation for everyone.

Another benefit of having engaged and loyal employees is that they become huge advocates for the Company. They're protective towards the Company because this is where they see their future.

For instance, recently one of my employees called me. He was working on a commercial property and the manager mentioned a big project they were planning. The employee went home, wrote a full report, and sent it to me by email. He included pictures, described what the job would entail, and how much time he thought it was going to take. He did this on his own time. I was very impressed by his initiative because it shows that he cares about the Company's growth and future. You create this kind of loyalty by trusting and investing in the employees.

And that brings me to a topic I consider to be fundamental in a creating a great workforce...

Investing in Your Employees

The word "invest" is sometimes misunderstood because people automatically assume that money is involved. Sometimes that is so, but "investment" can also be in terms of time, effort, and energy. In our company, we do spend money on the employees; for instance, by training them, but even more so, by providing opportunities for them to grow, to further their skills, and to advance through in-house training opportunities.

My experience has been that when you have your employees' back, they'll have your back too.

I have an employee who has been a good worker and who not only performs all his duties, but also goes the extra mile. Before I hired him, he told me he wasn't sure if he would be staying in this industry. His attitude and honesty were so refreshing that I hired him as a casual. He loved the potential in our company, loved the work and made the decision to stay and get trained. It turned out the more he grew with the company, the more invested in our company he became.

I see several reasons why investing in employees "pays off:"

1. It creates loyalty and engagement
2. Improves morale and satisfaction
3. Increases retention rates
4. Improves performance and productivity
5. Yields higher sales and profits
6. It creates company niches

You'll certainly want to invest in your employees if you consider what can happen if you are an uninterested boss. Employees know when you want the best for them instead of just for yourself.

Instead of having a committed and dedicated workforce, you'll end up with employees who are uninterested that don't give a hoot about their jobs, the Company, or your customers. And instead of making profits and growing your business, you will lose money.

I have heard from many other business owners that do not invest in training that their employees are always moving around. The employees do their job well and want to do more with their company, but the Company wants them to stay in that position. After a bit the employee will develop a wondering eye just so they can feel inspired again. They feel no attachment to their current position or the Company they work for and start to have no interest in its growth all because the Company didn't have an interest in their growth. Growth is a natural part of what inspires us and without it employees may lose interest and call in sick, become disengaged and eventually stop showing up for work.

When you have an employee that is feeling disempowered or not valued, you may notice their sick time increasing, their morale going down, and jobs not getting completed. Then you notice your profit dips and frustration sets in with both the employee and management. Now you might have to replace this person, the next thing you know your stress levels are increasing. This lack of mentality comes from a place of fear that if an employee grows they will move on and in the end they do anyway.

Obviously, this is not the kind of company that is going to be successful in the long run.

It is much more beneficial for everyone involved to set up your company with policies that allow employees to have input and make decisions.

You encourage decision-making in the employees. You create a culture that supports empowered employees. You get your team looking out for the Company's best interest, and then you have a policy for implementing the improvements that the employees suggest. Your employees are making your job as an owner so much easier. And there is something to be said about good intentions, from the management and the employees alike.

In any company, there's a lot of decision-making. How do you start categorizing the type of decisions that come up? One of the things that I always review each day with our employees is the intention for the day: "What is the intention for this job or for this day?"

If your intention is to get through it quickly and get home, then that might not be the best intention for the day. So, I always ask "What is the best way for them to be for the Company, for themselves, and for the customer?" Everyone comes to work with different things on their mind, they might be good for work or they might be bad. It doesn't help the Company if they are consumed with personal problems not remembering why they are at work and what is important about their job.

Depending on what your business is, the right headspace could be critical. If you have an employee who comes to work, and they've had a bad night and they're cranky, then you must remind them that the way they show up to work is a choice and to make the decision to leave their personal stuff at the door just for the 8 hours that they are at work. This is easier than it sounds and will help maintain good morale at work.

Another important point: I found it very important as a business owner to have a process or daily actions that I do so that I stay on track. They should be motivating and involve the actions you need to take to create an energized, productive, prosperous great day.

Critical Daily Actions

1. Create a **routine** first thing in the morning that sets your day up so that you look forward to your day - Meditation, affirmations, stretching or exercise.

2. Set daily **intentions** - Decide what kind of day you want to have no matter what happens, create a personal statement and declare it, i.e.; I will have a great day! I am a productive high-performance leader! I will create magic today!

3. With your team, have clear **communications** - Who is doing what, who is working with who, who is best suited for the job. My role is to give clear communication, make sure they have the tools they need to do the job, and encourage customer relations.

4. Start your day to be as smooth as possible. **Action Plan** - What is best for team and for customers. Limit room for error, fill in the daily planner sheet every morning!

"My philosophy is that not only are you responsible for your life but doing the best at this moment puts you in the best place for the next moment."

Oprah Winfrey

In this chapter, we have talked about hiring the right employee for your needs and how to ensure that you are a great employer/boss and leader. We also discussed some reasons why having engaged and loyal employees and empowering them will benefit you and your company.

Here's a quick summary of the main points:

- My path to becoming a stronger leader
- Respecting and appreciating your employees
- Empowering your employees to create loyalty and engagement
- Encouraging your employees to make decisions
- Importance of Guidelines and Procedure to follow
- Why have a chain of command?

- Communication
- Mistakes are part of growth
- Employee investment – why do it?
- Critical Daily Actions

The day that I took back control of how I was feeling about our company changed everything. I was no longer a victim of our employees; I was back in the driver seat. Nobody asked me to give up control, I handed it away. I got so caught up in the problems and the struggle that I forgot to be the solution. I forgot to use all the tools, skills and training that I had. I was not being a good leader and I was hurting the Company; the employees were just responding to the leadership style that was being provided to them.

"Success is still dreaming and feeling positive in the unfolding."
Abraham Hicks

Every time something happens good or bad in our company, I do a personal reflection on how we can celebrate and expand on it or how we could have prevented it, handled the situation better or differently. If a job goes south, what could I have done to prevent that from happening? Even if I am not directly involved I am responsible, because at the end of the day it is our company. If an employee has something to say, it is important to pay attention and to reflect on what is the best way to change or add ways of working with our employees to prevent or enhance whatever the situation is.

Our leadership is what makes the difference every time. Whenever something happens, there is usually something that we could have done differently that would have softened the blow or would have completely prevented it. My daily reflection process is an extremely important part of how the company moves forward creating the changes that are required. This process provides me with the mindset to be able to reflect and have the calmness to see things just as they are without conflicting emotions clouding the situation.

In Chapter 3, we will continue with this subject by exploring the importance of employee training.

Chapter 3:
THE IMPORTANCE OF TRAINING

WHEN I'M LOOKING FOR employees, I ask potential employees how they view doing a job they know they will probably need help with. Do they see problems, or do they see solutions? Do they see a learning curve, but still something they'd be willing to try or are they the type of person to freeze, freak out and say, "No, I can't do this"? How they react tells me a lot about how they will deal with stress and what their mindset will be on the job.

I hire the person who sees possibility and solutions over the person who might have more skill but less coping skills. I want the person that's more adaptable, flexible, motivated, and positive so when/if something happens that they are unprepared for, they have the right approach to resolve it.

In developing your high-performance team, look for people you can develop that also have the desire to grow. Training and development or growth are a must if you want to have a capable workforce. Helping our employees find a path that excites them, having them explore possibilities while developing a training plan is exciting for both the employee and the company.

This is why I now only hire someone who may not have the actual skills I'm looking for, but is adaptable, flexible, motivated, positive, and has the desire to grow.

There are some businesses and industries that do require their employees have certificates, degrees, etc. which may have taken them years to acquire. In some roles a certain standard of education and skills must be met. Depending on the type of business you have and the roles you are filling, if you are looking to hire trained or untrained employees, you combine their credentials with a great attitude and always hire to fit your culture.

In a nutshell, I hire people who have / are:

- Positive mindset
- Willing to go the extra mile
- Energy, enthusiasm
- Discussions about difference of opinion and how they resolve it (team co-operation)
- Maturity
- Team player (what does high-performance mean to them)
- Ability to follow policies
- Trust
- Ability to work towards a stretch goal and not feel overwhelmed but feel excited
- Focused on vision and mission

We say, "If this is something you want, and it inspires you, here is your path. You still must do your time, but just know that the opportunity is there. We'll train you along the way to help you get there."

This all starts with a conversation and a commitment from both our employee and management that says we are both invested in their growth. Some employees may think we can read their minds or interpret a conversation, "Well, they (my employer) should know this. I told them in a fleeting moment that, 'Yeah, I want to do that someday.'" Sit down and have a direct, clear conversation about their intentions and what you can do for and with them. Make sure your employees know what you are expecting, don't assume that they know.

Our employees have to want it and show initiative. There must be a goal or vision for them such as, "I am committed, and I want this growth," or "I want this change," and be willing to do the work to get there. As long as you provide them the path, you should encourage them to grow.

Meet face to face with your employee to ensure their growth is in alignment with your company's. Are they a team player? Review their past performance and ask questions without directing them. If you direct them, they will say what they want you to hear, whereas if you ask open-ended questions, "What will this training do for you?" You'll discover who they are and what their big dreams are with or without your company.

Operating your business under your normal daily operations, you may notice that your business is quietly slowing down to the point that it has come to a standstill. You may have long term employees at the top that are not leaving, and they are no longer self-motivated. You must find ways to grow your business or expand into new areas, so you can reenergize your current employees and hire additional employees to grow beyond your norm. This will create more opportunity and will separate your company from those that are on your heels wanting the business that you do have. If your business is stable and growth has slowed down, opportunities for your employees have also slowed down and they will notice this.

Create an environment keeping all your employees up to speed with your industry and then go one step further and become leading edge in the market place so you can take the lead in the industry. Improve, innovate and grow to show real impact. Improve faster than your competitors. Your alternative is to stay the same and have your competitors catch up and drive over you. Training will motivate your teams to performance excellence. Your services may not change but how your employees work and how your customers receive your services changes.

If you are not continually improving, your company will fall behind.

"Whether you think you can or think you can't, you're right!"
Henry Ford

Expanding Your Employees' Knowledge Base

The downfall in many businesses is thinking, "Oh, this person knows how to do this." They put the value on the skill set or existing training, more so than on the person that they're hiring.

Many companies are fearful of expanding the knowledge of their employees. They're afraid that if they invest in them, employees will leave for a better job. We have only experienced this a couple of times in the past and both times there was a plan put in place for their departure. In the end it has always worked out to be the best for the employee and the Company. I have never regretted being the type of employer who wants the best for our crew and shows them that there is so much more for them if they want it. More times than not, the employees value that in the Company and stay. Those who leave never would have stayed trained or untrained. We've had employees come and go for various reasons, but not because of training they received or lack of training or from broken promises.

Don't be afraid to train your employees so they can develop and continue contributing to the Company's growth. If they do the same thing every day, they may eventually get bored. If they're never challenged or given something new to engage their creativity, the employees may think, "If this is all this job has to offer, I may have to reevaluate whether I want to stay or move on."

"Worrying is using your imagination to create something that you don't want."

Abraham Hicks

I encourage my employees to share their goals with me. If they have a dream of doing something specific within this Company and they show me that they're willing to put in the time and work, then I'm 100 percent behind training them so that they can grow, help the Company grow, and continue to feel inspired.

I know of many companies that will bring in 3rd party companies to do different jobs. I much prefer to train my in-house staff to start doing those jobs, unless it's the kind of work that the Company decides it is not interested in pursuing. You keep the money in the Company. You keep your employees inspired, and you're growing your business.

Encourage Your Employees to Grow and Show Them the Way to Achieve It

Our employees know that there are learning opportunities available to those who wish to expand their expertise and knowledge base. Many will actually come to me asking how they can go to the next level, learn a specific skill, or ask what options are available for them to improve and grow within our company. It's a two-way street as they ask, and I offer.

If an employee was hired for a certain position but is motivated to do something more complex and they show me that they have what it takes, I am always willing to invest in training them.

This process starts with a conversation and a commitment from the employee as well as a commitment from us that we are invested in their growth. This is one of those moments when the aforementioned communication skills come in handy: sit down and have a direct, clear conversation about what their intentions are and what you can do for and with them, and what kind of commitment the Company needs from the employee to move forward with higher training.

I've learned to distinguish between those who have a real potential to grow and those that just blurt out the words who don't really want it. It's not enough for employees to tell you they want it; they have to show they can do it. There must be a goal or vision for them where they say, "I am committed, and I want this growth," or "I want this change," and then be willing to do the work to get there. You can see their willingness in everything they do for you and the Company on a daily basis. We also have stepping stone jobs that will show you they have the ability to do this training. You also get to see how they handle their current position while they wait for their training.

I'm cautious of people who tell me they have trainings unrelated to what my company does. If they think this job is a mere stepping stone while waiting for their career to start elsewhere, I am typically not interested. I also don't want to invest lots of time and resources in training somebody who wants to collect training certificates at my expense to add to their portfolio only to leave as soon as another opportunity comes their way. Your first clue should be when a job candidate tells you: "I just need to fill in some time before I get another job." Even if you hire temp or short-term workers, those are not the people you want to be training! It's like throwing good money away and you will not see the return on this investment. Part of the process I go through before I agree to upgrade someone with training is talking to their supervisors. Most employees do talk about their future plans with their working supervisors and you will learn a lot if you ask them about their work ethic, their drive, their abilities and if they are a promising candidate for continued trainings to use in your company.

If you have an employee you don't want to invest in, ask yourself why they are still working for you.

We had this one employee that was great, he grew, he did great work and he loved working at our company until the day he didn't. We noticed a shift in his attitude, we tried working with him, but he was unwilling to let go of some personal jealousies that overlapped into the Company affecting his work and his colleagues work environment. This guy also wanted additional training and with the noticeable shift in attitude, he was no longer a good fit for our training program. Once we made the decision that we would not provide continued training for him for one year to see if he could move past what he had going on, everything ended. He was not willing to wait and we where not willing to invest in someone with a bad attitude even though we knew he was trained well and was good at what he did.

Start Seeing Paid Training as a Worthy Investment

No business owner, myself included, is willing to part with their hard-earned money without a good reason. You might be thinking, "How much will this training cost? Or, "How much work will the employee miss costing me jobs while completing this training?" Those are all reasonable questions since no organization wants to lose profit while training its workers. However, in such cases it is important to look beyond these immediate concerns and focus on future benefits: How having a well-trained workforce will help the Company flourish and grow, not just financially, but also by creating satisfied and loyal workers who will actually care about the Company and its customers. Seen from this perspective, investment in training will certainly pay for itself many times over.

I've witnessed this often: If you value your employee and show your appreciation by investing in their growth and development, you will strengthen their commitment to your company and their future in it. In my experience, once employees feel valued, their performance and productivity increase.

I found that investment in training yields several benefits:

- Business runs better
- Employees have greater job satisfaction
- Employee retention creates loyalty and commitment to the Company
- You have more skills within your Company
- Employees share their expertise to help each other
- Employees have more ways to contribute
- They process their work differently and more effectively; they're better at problem-solving/solution-seeking and collaboration
- They can innovate to find better ways to do their job
- They feel the Company believes in them, they contribute and give back to the Company
- The customer experiences improve
- Jobs are completed better and faster
- Company's profits increase
- Your Company becomes the experts in the industry – you are leading the industry

Because we believe in the value of investing in our employees, we are spending a considerable amount of money on specialized training. None of our competitors have done this. Not only do we invest more in training, but we also approach this process differently. We know that skipping training courses to do hands-on, "trial-and-error training" results in substandard safety that creates safety hazards and concerns; we do not operate that way. This way of thinking is not in alignment with being leading edge experts bringing the best of what we do to the industry.

Instead, we train with specialized gear and use certification levels that are checked and renewed on a regular schedule. This gives our company a leading edge in our industry and peace of mind knowing that everyone is qualified and has the proper training to do their job at an expert level.

Yes, this approach has definitely cost us money, and it will continue to cost us because there's an upgrade and maintenance component. But the work that we're doing has opened up a lot of doors and continues to open up many more doors for us, precisely because we approach jobs differently from those that aren't well-trained. Our crews are now seen as more professional industry experts, because of their training and how they do their jobs compared to our competitors. We have expanded the type of jobs we can now do that our competitors do not have the skill level to do and these jobs pay well.

A few years ago, we decided to invest in becoming the leading-edge experts in our industry. We asked ourselves what that meant, how we could become known as the industry's best and how this would benefit our company.

This is what we found:

- Investing in training has provided our company with best practices, which sets us apart from our competitors. We have the industry best practices, we are the experts!

- Our crews are more efficient because of their training

- We do difficult jobs that our competitors cannot

- We can do more, be cost-effective for our clients, pay our employees well, and the Company makes more money.
- Our employees and our customers trust us
- Our employees are proud of what they can do
- We have a clear mission statement, it provides a vision and direction for making better decisions for the Company

If you're going to be the best, don't waffle in your decision; just be the best, which means do your best and give your best, you have to be the one to just do it! When running a business, there are many areas that you could be indecisive in but when you make the decision to be the leading-edge high-performance experts in your industry those decisions become black and white, it is either yes, we need that or no we do not. Being leading edge high performance experts makes those decisions clear.

Many business owners may think, "Well, if I'm to be the best leading-edge high-performance expert, how will I fit this in, I am so busy now and this feels like work." It is not more work, you are energized, more productive and you have less stress. You become the best by adopting steps that will support your company's growth and your employee's growth. You plan, invest, and act on these steps.

We have the edge in our company because we the owners decided to be the best, to get better jobs because we work in the absolute safest way getting more challenging jobs that pay very well. Customers do not want problems or unsafe practices on their property. When you can prove that your methods are the safest and you are the best in the industry, you will be taken very seriously.

Here's the flipside: if you don't provide training, new employees will learn bad habits, customers will complain, you will have safety concerns and you will damage your brand.

When we first started in this industry one of our competitors was known as the biggest company but didn't have a great street reputation. When I made the switch, and decided to become a high-performance leader, I also decided that I was going to build the best leading-edge company with teams of experts in this industry. If I was going to do this, I was going to do it to the best of my ability. We had quite the hill to climb and we are able to say that we did it. Our competitor was once known as the biggest is no longer and their street reputation has only gotten worse. I can only assume that the owners of that company did not pay attention and are not paying attention to what is happening in their company with their employees or to the shift in the industry. This did not happen overnight, but it did happen and there is now a noticeable difference between the 2 companies. My message here, is that you must always pay attention, don't let your success or your ego become a default to not paying attention so that your competitor can drive right past you.

"High performers are more successful than their peers, yet they are less stressed."

Brendon Burchard

Educate yourself and become the best at what you do, learn the ways of becoming a high performer and become a high-performance leader and teach your teams how to be that as well. There is always room to be and do better even if you're a top representative in your industry. Learn high performance leadership skills, add new techniques that will improve how you show up and what you are currently doing. You can ALWAYS expand and improve.

Show Your Employees Their Potential

Some workers know they have what it takes to advance their skills and they'll come to you and ask for training. Others may have the same potential to improve their know-how but perhaps don't recognize it themselves.

This is where you, as an employer, can help.

Timing is also vital, as the following example shows:

Freddy has been with us just over a year now. He's a terrific guy with a great attitude. He's quiet, somewhat laid back, and doesn't always express himself, but does excellent work. When he first started working for us, before he had any experience, he said he wanted to be hanging off ropes. As I would tell anybody, "You get your feet wet, show me your interest, and we'll lead you in that direction."

A few times Freddy had the opportunity to do some rope work in a controlled environment. These were safety procedures that we run sporadically during the year. Employees learn how to climb up ropes, how to perform personal and employee rescues, and get some height experience under their belt.

However, Freddy decided not to participate in these procedures. My interpretation was that he had lost interest. He was given an opportunity, he was there, but he walked away from it. Later, I said to him, "You told us you were interested, but when you had an opportunity to try it, you walked away. Am I to interpret that you're not interested in ropes anymore?"

He said he still was, so I talked to him about it. It turned out that because he was still relatively new in the Company, he wasn't very confident. Although he had a desire to try something new, the timing wasn't right. But because he was interested and committed, his path was laid out for him. Next year, when he is more confident and "seasoned," we'll train him on the ropes.

This is another, important aspect of training: employees must be able to ask for what they want, and the timing must be right. Training someone who is not ready for this work will surely backfire.

What if, despite your good intentions, the employee just doesn't work out?

I've always found it best to be slow to hire and when warranted quick to fire. Most of your competition will probably be quick to hire and slow to fire. That was a trait that we also use to get caught in.

You may think a bad employee is better than no employee. I found it not to be the case. It works out when you make the space to allow somebody new to show up, they will.

When we first bought this company, every employee we had came from the old company and they brought with them tons of baggage and attitude about the Company and their job. We experienced in-house turmoil, bad employee morale, and bad habits. You could feel the negativity and tension within the group. I just thought, "What did we get involved with here?"

We tolerated it for the first bit but once we gained more experience and started to make adjustments, many employees left. The second year, we had a better crew, some new and still some of the original team, things did get better but even then, they were still bringing their old bad habits to the Company and on job sites.

I got caught with one employee thinking "I can't let him go". We had the worst six months ever. I knew bad things were going on, but I thought, "Who will do this job if we let him go, we don't know how to do this?"

"We are what we repeatedly do. Excellence then, is not an act, but a habit."

Aristotle

We finally changed all that around.

Take the leap, let them go and trust, "I'm trusting that some-one will show up". I did let him go and trusted that the right person would show up, and they did. The second he left, I felt huge relief. I did not realize until he was gone the unspoken continual stress that I was feeling and holding onto every day. New happy candidates showed up once the toxic employee was gone, people who wanted to work for us became great team members.

We took the leap. The right people showed up. I have learned over the years they always show up.

"Fear will keep us doing what we don't want."
Susan Delano Swim

In this chapter I talked about the importance of hiring an employee with a great attitude and the advantage of training your employees to expand your employees' skills and knowledge base for your benefit and theirs.

Here's a quick summary of the main points:

- Type of person I hire
- Mindset - positive or negative, is it a big deal?
- Attitude Versus Skill
- Training - Investment - Benefits
- Employee growth and how to achieve it
- Be the best in your industry
- Trust what you need to do

When you make the decision that your company is to be the best in your industry and you and your employees are trained to be high-performance experts, the Company's morale improves, and you are on your way to be the industry experts. By stating and owning that you are the best in your industry, you will change how you do business. If you are the best and truly own that, you will change your daily actions, you will want to learn more, be more, do more and be the absolute best to be the most professional no matter what industry you are in. Being leading edge industry experts means you are continually pushing the envelope to be and do better. It is a never-ending learning and growth path because there are always other businesses on your coat tails and you must continue your growth to continue to be the best, to be the leading-edge industry experts. This may sound like work but once you are in the flow of being a high performer, this way becomes natural and exciting because you can feel the growth and the growth shows in your profits. Being proud of your accomplishments and where you are headed being a leading-edge company is extremely rewarding and exciting and I am assuming that is why you went into business in the first place. Status quo is not exciting and can be depressing; there are no business incentives if nothing is new to look forward to. If you are not creating new ways of being and doing your business, your competitor may just slip by you because they decided to be the high performance leading experts in your industry. Make a conscious decision every day to be excited about your business, to be the leading edge high performance company and see what changes.

In Chapter 4, we'll explore another very useful topic: How to create collaboration and synergy among your employees.

Chapter 4:
CREATE COLLABORATION AND SYNERGY AMONG EMPLOYEES

COLLABORATION AND SYNERGY MEANS the com-
bined energy and effort among your employees, management,
the company as a whole. When each individual and division
collaborates and works together, you will achieve better results
while knowing there is a support system in place to support the
Company's needs.   Creating an environment of collaboration
and synergy makes for a feel-good work place where the productivity as a group will outperform any one person's efforts making
the company more money.

With collaboration and synergy, you create a better business.
Creating and encouraging your teams to work well together
equals great synergy and will open creative pathways for your
employees to do more and have a better outcome from their
experience. Your teams will form a synergistic relationship just
by working with all the talents within the Company, this is a
crucial part of the bigger picture.

For example, we run in-house trainings and one of the best-
run trainings that we've had in our company lasted ten-hours.
Although it was a long day, it was interactive, engaging and the
trainer made an effort to connect with each participant. Everybody was receptive to the information, all employees trained with

different team members from their norm and all where in great spirits, which made it a fantastic experience, which turned into the employees looking forward to all future trainings.

When the participants and trainer are comfortable, upbeat and excited, and the employees enjoy working with each other, collaborating, they will be more interactive and will retain the information better. We've had trainings before where someone was in a bad mood, and this one person changed the group dynamic and the dynamic of the presenter. One person's negative energy will affect the atmosphere of the training session which in turn affects all the participants.

When positive energy is not present, information gets lost.

Create Synergy & Collaboration:

- Sharing knowledge, best practices, different perspectives
- Keeping jobs in-house = more profit
- Increased employee morale: showing their expertise, they develop trust and know each other's skills
- Customers call you for other jobs to see if you can help them
- Great for business to respond to job opportunities to improve and enhance the company's growth
- Employees know they have support and can count on each other
- Employees have someone to bounce ideas off
- Employees don't feel the pressure of being on their own

"Synergy is better than my way or your way. It's our way."
Stephen Covey

As the Leader, You Affect Everyone Below You

Your leadership style creates the Company's work culture!

The leaders' energy flows down to the employees and is one of several possible elements that can impact an employee's experience. They can be either nervous or not engaged because you're moody, or they're happy and productive because you're emitting a positive uplifting attitude. You may be having a rotten day but your job as a leader is to manage your emotional state. Your job as a leader is to lead in the best possible way to set your employees up to have the best experience possible for that day.

What is your role in this?

- Demonstrate your commitment to the Company

- Lead by example

- Encourage all employees in all aspects of the Company

- Create collaboration between the supervisors/management and the team

- Encourage supervisors to participate in processes and get ideas for the best outcomes possible

- Learn how to work best with supervisors and employees to teach them new ways of doing things

- Be transparent and honest

- Delegate, trust, communicate

- Be authentic, create connections, speak directly, show enthusiasm

- Keep an upbeat attitude, encourage morale

- Be accountable, keep your word

- Act ethically and responsibly

As a leader, you are responsible for your mood, your demeanor, and setting the workplace atmosphere. Everything you do affects everyone else. You can have a bad day, but if you have repetitive bad days, you will impact the Company's synergy. Your employees won't thrive or even come to you with questions or concerns because they don't want to create more problems AND they don't want to hear your problems,

So how can you set the right mood? It's all about daily practices that will keep you in top shape as a high-performance leader:

- Have a daily routine that sets you up to be in the best mindset, to have clarity for how your day will go and to know what is important to you

- Set daily intentions, remind yourself of the best possible outcomes during your day

- Pay attention to yourself, check in on your thoughts and how you are feeling several times during the day

- Take time-outs to clear your thoughts and re-energize

- Ask yourself every day, "How can I improve my leadership today?", "How am I living today?" This question does affect your work — how you are living is about everything you do and don't do all the time and the underlying feeling that you have.

Every day I come to work, I always remember it's a fresh start. Everything and anything is possible! Anything personal that I have going on stays outside my office door. It does not come into my office, affect my customers or my employees. I schedule regular personal awareness check-ins to make sure my emotions and thoughts are not lost and overflowing. Even though who you are shows up everywhere with everything that you do, there are parts that do not belong at work. That is why I do check-ins: to make sure that when I am having a tough personal time, my professional space does not feel it and is not affected by it.

If there is a day that I need to push myself, I will say one of my power statements that will make the shift I am looking for, i.e. "I am a high-performance leader" or "I am creative, resourceful and whole, I can do this!". When I say one of those statements, it creates a shift that I need to be that person. If I am having the type of day where time is just moving along, I ask myself, "How am I living today?" This question catches me every time raising my level of awareness for what I am doing as I always strive to be and do my best, especially in challenging situations. If I don't feel that I am living that day, I am just existing and working, I will shift how I am working by doing one of my exercises. It is the shift that I need which will create a happier me which creates better business.

If you walk in your office door thinking, "Oh, I'm so angry, too much bad stuff is going on right now," or saying, "I am so stressed out," then that's how you're going to show up and react to everything that happens during your day. Before I implemented my routines and practices, I would just show up to work, put my head down and start. My days where stressful but manageable, I had no self-awareness routines or check in's in place, I just had stuff to do and most of the time I felt pulled in multiple directions trying to manage this the best I could. Unfortunately, this is how most business owners operate, this has become their norm not realizing that there is a much simpler more fulfilling way to do your work.

In other words, your mindset determines how you will run your business each day and will impact every single decision you make. Maintain self-awareness and keep your mindset focused and unwavering with your intentions on how you want to be and what you are creating at work.

You create the energy that you bring into the office. If you feel unhappy or exhausted, you drain the surrounding environment in the Company. Most people think if they need a boost to get coffee, they will get an increase in their energy, but it's <u>not</u> <u>about caffeine</u>. Learning how to naturally keep your energy up and having thought awareness knowing how to create positive thoughts / vibrations, will result in a more sustainable, energized productive day = happier work environment.

Build your energy as a leader in the workplace:

- Brain breaks: stop what you are doing every 60 minutes, stop thinking about your project at hand for five or ten minutes, reenergize yourself, and your end result will be considerably better.

- Shift your focus during your brain breaks – look out or go outside if you can, notice and appreciate all the surrounding areas natural beauty, drink a glass of water, practice a mini-meditation, talk to a colleague or a family member. Move – go for a walk, stretch, take deep breaths, take a break

- Focus on one task at a time. Multi-tasking is not a real thing, it creates half thought out work and is mentally draining to constantly be shifting your thoughts

- Turn off all social media and put your phones on hold for scheduled times so you can focus on your project at hand.

The point about moving around and stretching is certainly important. I used to have the "ass in chair" syndrome, sitting at my desk all day long, every day. Being sedentary affects your energy, making you listless, both physically and mentally and starts to affect your overall health. Sitting is now recognized to be as bad for you as smoking.

One of the best ways I found to increase my energy is to have a stopwatch by my computer. Every 60 minutes it goes off, I get up and move. I go get a drink of water, go talk to somebody, or go in another room and take some deep breaths and stretch. I move and stop thinking about what I'm doing so I can have a brain break for a few minutes.

When I come back, I am recharged, I have a new perspective and inspiration, I cultivate new ideas to complete what I was doing, and I feel completely refreshed.

If we stop doing whatever it is we're doing to give ourselves a brain break, we think better, we work better, and we create the space to allow new ideas to emerge which makes us better at our job. Creation comes from allowing space.

Do You Have a Bunch of Employees or Do You Have a Team?

Having a team cultivates a stronger workforce rather than having employees working individually. A well-organized team sparks creativity and is a good support system. It will increase your income because you have different resources and strengths working together.

A team ensures a more empowered way of working and puts everyone on an equal playing field as far as expertise goes, each skill is as important as the other in accomplishing the task at hand. It also creates instant support and spirit in their work community.

To form a team:

1. You need a qualified, experienced trainable leader (first in communication to the team)

2. Inform all team members that he/she is their go-to person

3. Have a policy in place for problem-solving / solution seeking on job sites or with other employees to avoid guesswork

4. Teams must have work quality and performance expectations led and expressed by the supervisor

5. Timeline expectations are extremely important for your productivity and bottom line

The leader determines who is part of each team, when teams should be changed, and how the team will function, so everyone feels safe and valued. The team atmosphere encourages everyone to communicate and work together.

Set up a supportive, friendly, and nonjudgmental environment:

- Have the right staff and equipment to do the job
- Make everyone accountable
- Be organized
- Encourage employee contribution and input
- Lead by example
- Be clear with your employees so there's no miscommunication
- Be flexible and open
- Always tell them how much you appreciate them
- Tell them the value they bring to your organization
- Let go of toxic employees

For people to work well with their colleagues, there must be trust and camaraderie. Then it's a matter of feeling comfortable and safe expressing yourself, knowing that you're heard, and you're not going to be ridiculed or judged because somebody didn't like what you had to say.

When you set up a supportive environment, employees feel like they don't have to be isolated, they can collaborate.

"Coming together is a beginning. Keeping together is progress. Working together is success."

Henry Ford

Your Team's Strengths

If your employees don't feel safe to express what they know and what they're capable of doing, then nobody ever knows what in-house resources you have. They may think that they can sort of do a certain job not knowing that their colleague has a lot of experience doing that same job.

Knowing what everyone's strengths are is what creates a community of support so that the Company doesn't always rely on enlisting third parties. Outsourcing costs more money than delegating the work to someone in the Company who has that specific skill. Recognizing your employee's additional skill sets mean you recognize them and the additional value they bring to the Company.

We have employees that are certified bricklayers, certified masons, professional painters, professional window installers/ glazers, many of them coming from other trades, bringing their expertise and experience. They're no longer doing that trade, but if there's a job where that skill is required, we have skilled trades people available.

We don't have people here just doing a job. They are advancing our company's vision. They all like working here, they like their job and our style of leadership.

"The strength of the team is each individual member. The strength of each member is the team."

Phil Jackson

On many occasions, our staff will call wanting to do a job that is a stretch for them, we trust our employees to know that when they say they can do a different type of job that they can do it and do it well.

Your employees are solving problems for customers. They bring the solution to you, you tell the customer you can do that, and you set the price. At the end of the day, your employees are solution seekers, creating great customer service and loyalty, while making money for the Company by creating team support.

How to do this:

- **Mission Statement** - an important part of our daily expression and vision of the Company. Our daily activities must be in alignment with it, so we are representing the company in the best way possible and headed in the right direction

- **Expectations / Impressions** - I share with our employees what my expectations are, and I have them state what theirs are. I express the importance of first impressions so that our customers like and trust us right away knowing that everything they do is part of the customer experience

- **Employee / Customer interactions** - every interaction leaves our employees and our customers with a feeling. Did we take care of them, did they feel heard, did they feel the value for the service they received? Were we proactive / preventative to future issues? Did our employees feel great while doing their job?

- **Management is proactive** - we play a role knowing the job sites our employees are working on. We aim to be proactive to all possible situations, so they know ahead what to expect, to be prepared and to have all the equipment required for the job

- **Collaborative Team Support** - all team members know who to call for the support they need for different situations
- **Our employees will call with referrals** for extra work they see on a neighbouring site. We offer a financial benefit to employees if they are successful getting the Company new customers.
- **Our supervisors carry business/sales cards** to distribute to new opportunities if they see a job that we can bid on. If this is successful, they will get rewarded

When people work as a team, they look out for the best interest of the Company, creating a culture of growth and opportunity. Your energy will flow out to the organization and to everybody in it.

I call this the "culture of thriving," which means creating the kind of environment that encourages creativity and innovation in all areas of the Company. This means:

- All your employees want to show up to work even if there are challenges or difficulties
- Transparency and employee freedom will attract more employees. Your policies and procedures guide your employee culture
- Hire those who fit your culture
- Share your mission and vision for your company
- Have your employees contribute, so they will feel valued and feel like they are part of a team

A thriving culture is crucial. I make most of my decisions based on how things feel. If I feel the Company does not have a feeling of thriving and being a happy place, then I stop and see what the problem is before I go any further.

A company that is thriving creates more projects, more business, while having happier clients that refer our company or start engaging our company for additional projects. It creates positive relationships because your clients are being taken care of, your employees are happy, and your business is doing well.

This culture, in which people are creating magic daily and your customers are happy with the work, turns into dollars, because customers want more work done, your company is top of their mind. When there's a project, they will call and say, "Is this something that you can do for me?".

Creating magic everyday is easier than you think!

"Team synergy has an extraordinary impact on business results."

Patrick Lencioni

There's an exercise you can do where you flip a coin and if you get heads, that means today you are committed to creating magic, it changes your mindset for the day. If you flip tails, you have the option to pick a magical day or one that's your normal way of being, but you get to choose. This sounds simple but the results you get when you flip heads are profound. If you commit to the exercise and to creating a magical day, all the crap gets left behind. Ask yourself, "How can I create magic today?", you are now working outside your normal mindset, you start looking for ways to spark a difference. You will be happier and feel joy while working from a magical perspective opening creative pathways outside your normal thought box improving your work and your environment while having fun.

Once you do this exercise once, you will realize you have the power to create a happy, magical day every day just by shifting your perspective or flipping a coin.

It's All A Matter of Perspective

As you can see, thriving is a conscious decision; doing an exercise as simple as flipping a coin makes you more aware of your choice if you are someone who gravitates towards negativity or if you are someone that gets stuck working the same thought patterns over and over.

The coin is a simple reminder of your power to shape your day.

It is all a matter of perspective: Your world can change when you change your mindset. We get stuck in our own thoughts and have habitual behaviors. Learning to walk away, take a deep breath, and smell the roses can make all the difference in how you work on your projects or simply flip a coin and take a stance to make magic happen starting at that moment.

These are some of the ways to shift your perspective from a negative to positive one:

1. Be present, let go of the past and stop thinking you can control the future

2. Be open, rather than attached to just one view

3. Be grateful for this moment, write down three things that you are grateful for

4. Go for a walk

5. Take a break and eat a snack

6. Brain break – 5 – 10 minute meditation or just stop thinking about the task at hand

7. Talk to a colleague

8. Pay attention to your feelings, always work towards feeling good. Feeling bad and getting stuck with negative thoughts only creates negative reactions. When this happens ask yourself what thoughts will feel better?

9. Change your perspective to the opposite of the one you have, feel the relief and see what new ideas show up

10. ASK: How am I living today? This little question is very powerful and can take you to how you want to be, instead of what you fall into out of habit

11. Flip a coin - choose to create magic

One of the greatest tools we have is the ability to change our perspective at any given moment, regardless of the challenge. Many of us make work too hard by thinking that we must just get the work done; removing all possibilities of being creative, but creativity is what promotes growth in a company. Being in the heavy grind of the daily operations just to get it done is not as productive as you may think it is and is not the best way to have inspiration to create new business. Having brain space for creativity, being open to engaging your imagination, being happy in your company and remembering to create magic are the keys to success beyond the bump and grind.

"You must look within for value but must look beyond for perspective."

Denis Waitley

When You Keep It Simple, Work Can be Easy

Our teams do very physically demanding jobs. I get a much better outcome from my employees when they begin a job with the right perspective, such as, "Although this is a challenging project, I am up for this, I like to be challenged." There can be simplicity and job satisfaction depending on how you go about your work.

The leader can either make the job feel very complicated and difficult for their teams by how they view the job, or they can downplay the difficulty by finding the simpler solutions. Don't complicate things!

Our company's supervisors are directly involved with our teams. The supervisor's perspective affects management's view, which then trickles down to the team's perspective and, finally, to what the customer sees and feels. If the customer thinks that you're needlessly complicating the job, you might not get return calls. But if you approach all your jobs, simple and difficult ones, being motivated to serve your customer the best way possible by how you do your work and by doing it well, you will have a repeat customer.

Your employees should know why their job is important to them, why they work for your company and why you do what you do. This creates a deeper understanding about the company, knowing all of this will create a shift in their performance creating a powerful work force. This knowledge will increase employee loyalty, engagement and commitment dedicated to doing great work for your customers. They will understand why knowing this translates in their work performance, their job becomes more than just a job.

One simple exercise to shift your employee's perspective is to ask them to pretend they are the customer, ask them what they would expect, what they would want or what they would see in how they are performing. How great would you feel about the service that you are providing if you where on the receiving end paying the bill as one of your customers?

The lesson here is: don't complicate things. Simplify everything! When things feel complicated chances are you are probably really deep into the process and see it as being considerably more difficult than it actually is which is now causing you to become frustrated. Ask yourself what would be different if this was simple, what is best for the customer and you will get an answer.

Capitalize on Your Employees' Potential

As an employer, you always want to see great potential in your employees: their interests, ingenuity, and creativity to assist with finding solutions that others don't see.

I always keep in mind the following aspects:

- **Accountability:** No one is wrong. If something happens, employees should feel safe telling you. You don't want them to stop showing their potential because of one error or fear of one happening

- **Speed:** They work efficiently, find ways to continually improve and move on. Offer incentives for great work done within a certain timeframe

- **Talent/skill:** Everybody brings a certain talent with them. Encourage employees to use their talents and collaborate

- **Leaders:** We have supervisors in our company, but we also expect everyone to be personally responsible for their work

- **Creativity:** Ask your employees to see a different perspective, what is the best or simplest way to work efficiently and effectively while enjoying the job.

By capitalizing on your employees' potential, you'll have a high-performance team that creates vibrant energy and works efficiently. Their production will surpass your expectations, bringing excitement, the possibility of business expansion and profits.

"Alone we can do so little; together we can do so much."
Helen Keller

If you think of your team as just a team and yourself as just a leader or as their buddy, and you don't have expectations of professionalism along with expected deadlines in your work or theirs, then you are not being a high-performance leader and you are not capitalizing on your workforce's potential. If you don't expect anything from your employees; performance expectations, their opinion, no creativity, no input into the Company, then that is exactly what you will get. They will be or will become uninterested and will come to work and do their job without any motivation. They're not going to be their best, do their best or look for extra jobs for the Company because it isn't required of them and they are not self-motivated to care to do it. They may not tell you important information about their jobs because they're not invested in the Company. You may find yourself continually wanting to replace them, which is expensive and frustrating.

It's easy to take for granted that you can replace somebody. If I feel something is off with any of my employees, I take the time to figure out what the Company can do to support this employee to bring them back on track. You never know what's going on in somebody's mind. After working with them if things are not improving, and we feel that they are no longer filling their role or fitting in with the Company, we will let them go.

Get to know your employees. Engage them in what the Company values are, and they will feel like they belong.

When somebody shows up for an interview, start with the assumption, "This person is valuable and has potential that they'll contribute to the team." Tell them right from the start, "I want to know if you can see yourself doing this and if it feels natural and exciting for you. What other skills do you bring that will be an asset to the Company?"

One of our supervisor is leaving next year, so we've been looking for and grooming his replacement. Another employee has been with us for three years. Every year, he's outperformed himself and is really showing his potential. A couple of months ago he said, "Because the supervisor is leaving, I am seeing an opportunity here. I want to let you know that I will do everything I can to fill those shoes and to learn what I need to learn to do his job."

I have employees deciding how they want to be trained and grooming themselves. It's been happening that way for quite a few years. They see what we do, they see their potential and that we encourage training for their advancement, making space for where they want to grow.

Getting great new employees starts with being a great employer and knowing what to look for. We've had employees from our competitors' run-away pool that do not last. They cannot keep up with our fast pace and hard work, they do sloppy work and they all say our guys work too hard.

Needless to say, these individuals don't fit in with our employees or our culture. They end up returning to the competitor and getting their old jobs back with the same old habits, behaviors and mindsets. We inspire our teams by appreciation, opportunity and kindness.

I see the potential in our employees rather than the actual situation right in front of me. I see greatness, and when I see greatness that's been stripped away from our employees, there are different conversations that I'll have with them privately so that they have a choice to bring it back.

When you see your employees attitude shift and they are not living up to their true potential and then they catch it and shift back to being great, your company can't lose. I have seen employees experience moments where they get lost. I had one employee that I witnessed everything about him shifting. His work attitude shifted, the way he was talking to me, our management team, his team and colleagues also changed. In about three to four weeks, I was noticing and experiencing this shift. His co-workers were starting to complain about him. It can happen that fast. After I talked to him and explained what we were seeing and experiencing, it was a matter of moments before he brought himself back. Most of the time people don't realize how they are bringing their personal stuff to work, they think they are hiding their problems. A simple, kind, and caring conversation may be all it takes for the shift you are looking for.

The best thing you can do is keep your valuable employees. They are your company. But if you have an employee who is not conforming, who is just not fitting in, you may just have to let him go. If you are lucky, you will mutually agree that it is time to move on. Don't lower your standards or beg an employee to stay. Work with them until you realize your efforts are futile. It is important to deal with this the best way possible and to not let this drag on for months as your other employees will feel this and it could create a shift in them.

Make Your Employees Feel Heard

Businesses rely on communication, the exchange of ideas and information. I think it is the most important function of running a successful business: communication with your employees, your customers, and everyone involved with the running of the Company. It's not just letting someone speak, it must also involve listening, acknowledgment of what is being said, and appreciation of the employees and customers. This can be done either verbally, through rewards or written.

Appreciation is something that needs to be voiced all the time, in a very natural, authentic way. If you do it very sporadically or just once a year, it's not the same as being consistent in showing employees your appreciation for their role in your organization. It's natural for me to express and show this but it is not for everyone in the Company. Appreciation is something that I'm very consciously aware of that I talk about and acknowledge whenever I talk to my employees and customers.

Paying attention and listening to your employees you hear the unspoken and then you ask about it. I had a situation with an employee a while back. I could tell things weren't right. When I had a private conversation with him, it became clear that he had a lot of stuff going on privately that he was bringing to work. I gave him a few exercises to practice, he now knows he has a choice every day to decide what he brings to work and what he doesn't. I told him, "I know you don't want to bring your problems here and affect your colleagues. Let's find a practice that works for you so that you can leave this stuff where it belongs."

One of the exercises I gave this employee was the coin toss, this exercise made the decision for him. He could now let the coin decide what kind of day he was going to have: a joyful, productive, magical one, or one filled with anxiety and anger. Once he flipped the coin, it became very easy for him to make that choice, he was going to make magic.

I also suggested for him to hand write (no computer) all his thoughts down on a piece of paper, a stream of consciousness, and let it all out "the good, the bad and the ugly", when he feels some relief, have a ceremonial burial or burning of the piece of paper. Don't re-read it, do edit it, don't tuck it away, get rid of it, and if your thoughts get heavy again, repeat the exercise. He reported that this exercise worked extremely well for him.

If you don't listen or pay attention to your employees when they do bring their personal problems to work, their attitude will impact your company, and if done repeatedly you might lose a valuable employee just because something wasn't addressed.

All employee issues must be addressed in a timely manner or unintentional turmoil affecting others can happen.

7 Strategies to Paying Attention:

1. **Let your employee be heard**, give them time and space to express what is happening and keep the discussion about them

2. **Don't interrupt** – let them say what they need to say

3. **Agree** where you can agree and apologize where you should

4. **Observe** body language and emotional tone

5. **Be authentic** - only say what you are willing to do, don't rush to end the meeting and then have remorse

6. **Show appreciation** for the conversation, for their vulnerability and for working on a resolution

7. **Follow up**, schedule a check in conversation

Everyone Knows Where Their Place In the Company Is

If people come to work and don't really know what their job is or where they fit in the Company, a feeling of uneasiness arises. If they're consistently feeling that way, chances are they're looking for another job and might soon leave.

Depending on how much you value that employee, you might want them to move on. Maybe that's why they don't feel like they're part of the team. But if you don't want them to leave, you must make them feel like they're part of something. Embrace them, engage them, and hear what they have to say.

"Always treat your employees exactly as you want them to treat your best customers."

Stephen Covey

One of the things that will work well with your team is if there is structure in place and people know how to use it and respect it.

In our chain of command, which is something that we enforce to give everybody the chance to do their job properly, we have an operations manager who goes around and ensures that the jobs are set up with the right employees and the right supervisors.

The supervisors have their teams and it's the supervisor's job to ensure that the teams are confident and know what they're doing.

If we have a problem with one of the team members or they don't feel confident with one of their jobs, they know to go to the supervisor, not to call the operations manager, because the on-site supervisor is the problem-solver for that team.

If you have a team member who decides he wants to skip over the supervisor and go right to the operations manager, that will create a conflict because he is not asking the right person for support. If it's a problem where they feel they can't go to the supervisor, then that needs to be resolved through communication with the people involved.

If you find that the two people just can't work together, coach them so they can, and if that fails, find another team for this person to work on if you value them as an employee.

Creating a chain of command that people respect means everybody knows who to go to if there is a problem. Their supervisors are the first person to approach. If the supervisor can't resolve the problem, they can collaborate with the other team supervisors, if that doesn't resolve the problem, management is their back up. This takes the pressure off the owners to constantly be solving the problems. It puts the power back in the supervisor's hands, the employee and the team get the power to resolve issues without always phoning for support. Sometimes, people will get in the habit of (without even thinking) calling and saying, "I can't fix or do this!" When this happens, it is important to remind them to step back, reach out to the next person in the chain of command, and to review protocol so that this doesn't continue.

Whenever I'm training a new person, I will get them to call me in the beginning if they have a problem, but I don't solve the problem for them. I will ask them questions about how they can fix this situation on their own so that they can create or develop some self-confidence in what they're doing. This approach helps build their confidence so that they can do the job because I know that they have all the skills to do it.

Have confidence in your supervisor so that the team gels well. If the supervisor can't solve the problem, then he can ask another supervisor, "Have you experienced this? What is your best solution?" If nobody has, then guide them to keep going up the chain to find the answers they need, so they feel good about the job and the customer is happy. Supporting and keeping their confidence in what they are doing is a huge part of their success.

There's Value in Everyone Feeling Important

"Things here never change," or "nobody cares" are not good words to hear about your company or from your employees. We have built a company that constantly embraces change and provides new opportunities.

"Customers will never love a company until the employees love it first."

Simon Sinek

Our employees are happy to come to work. When I have a check-in call with my supervisors at the end of the day, I hear how well their day went and the solutions they came up with. They tell me about resolved issues and how they fixed them. Those are great days.

Employees say, "I'm not sure how I'm going to do this," or, "I don't think we can do this."

I say, "Okay, walk around the job site and just look at this. Get creative. How would you do something if you were to design it on your own terms while maintaining all safety regulations." "Look at this job from the customer's perspective, what is the best possible outcome you would want if you were the customer?" I often get a call back, "We can do it. We're going to do it this way."

We've had many jobs where things have been very challenging. The possible first reaction is, "Oh my. I don't know." But the moment you remove the fear and ask them to get creative and open their mind, they see possibilities rather than obstacles. They come back happy and proud of themselves for figuring this out. Get your employees to look at things differently.

For example, we were working on a very large house with a very slippery metal roofing. A couple of spots were difficult to access. Employees thought the only way that they could do their work was by bringing in a boom. However, a boom is expensive for the customer and can potentially damage their property.

Always, take a step back, walk around the site, and look for other possibilities, get creative. Use all your skills and think what is possible if we approach this from another side: "What if I was to come from the back of the house with ropes and come over the roof? What if I was to come from here, from there? How could I do this?" Jobs are never black and white, and I never want my employees to look at them that way.

Within half an hour, they called me back and said, "We have a plan. We can do this." There was no more expense for the Company or the customer and my employees where proud of themselves for implementing this plan. The customer got the quality job that they were seeking, and my employees were extremely happy because they figured it out. It's a huge win, win.

Here's a quick summary of the main points in this chapter:

- Importance of creating collaboration and synergy in your Company
- Leader creates everything below them
- Questions to ask yourself about your leadership style
- Creating the right mood

- Start fresh every day – your daily check in
- Creating a personal power statement and its importance
- You are what you think – there is no faking it
- Employees or a team
- Designating a leader
- Right person in the right position
- Mission statement
- Culture of thriving, the importance of creating magic
- Perspective check-ins
- Importance of simplicity
- Communication
- Chain of command
- Encouraging creativity at work

It is challenging to run a service industry business. What has been the most challenging aspect for us is managing our employees. We have great employees most of the time, and all it takes is one, sometimes the one you least expect, to throw you a curve ball. It can throw a wrench in your day starting at 6 am. It became very important for our survival and our stress levels to develop strong leadership and teams, so when something did happen, and it did, we could handle it easily, removing the stress out of it. As we all know, even the best laid out plans and executed projects have bumps along the way. When you develop your leadership style to that level, the bumps are smaller.

Being a high-performance leader is all about the practices that you engage in. These practices will make your life easier, more efficient, more proactive, more of everything that is good, and will give you more free time. Being a high-performer means your days are on purpose designed to get more of the important things completed. This will directly affect the daily operations of your company and, most importantly, affect the moral, in turn, your profits.

"The life I live is created by the story I tell."
Abraham Hicks

The stories that we tell ourselves both for our business relationships and our personal relationships are what are leading us. They are what we carry around, whether they are serving us or holding us back. I have heard clients say, "these are just my thoughts I don't say them or tell anyone." The problem with this statement is that your actions are from your thoughts; whether you think you are controlling them or not, they do affect you in one way or another.

Maybe you are exhausted or overwhelmed or have a lot of anxiety, maybe you feel stressed out or just plain beaten up by everything coming at you all the time. That is why it is so important to take the steps that will lead you in the direction that you want to go, the ones that will move you forward, the ones that make you feel great every day. After all, that is why we are here on earth - to feel joy every day doing what we must do. Feeling stressed out and becoming numb to the stress has unfortunately become the norm. That is why a high-performance lifestyle is so important. These habits give you back your downtime and most importantly you can feel joy at work and at home again.

In Chapter 5, we'll explore another important topic: how to align team directives with your business vision.

Chapter 5:
ALIGN THE TEAM DIRECTIVES
WITH YOUR BUSINESS VISION

A QUESTION I OFTEN ask myself, and it likely is of concern to you as well: How can we consistently improve to provide our customers with service that gives them the best possible outcome, while also ensuring our employees are having the best possible experience while doing their jobs?

To me, great customer service is based on my code of ethics: "Do unto others as you would have them to do unto you." In other words, give the customers what they want and then go one step further and add that special surprising touch. Our customers are extremely important people in our company; without them, we wouldn't have a business.

What's important to me is developing a relationship with our customers so that we are on the top of their mind when they require services that we offer. To achieve this, the Company must be accessible and flexible enough to meet all the demands that are requested of us and we must provide our customers with a great experience. Our employees know that our customers are our priority and we must always be respectful and communicate in a timely manner either on the phone or in-person.

Our policy is that our customers are always right, and we stand by that; we want them to know that they matter to us and they are not just another job. I want our customers to feel that we provide expertise, we respond to their needs, and the service we provide will exceed their expectations.

We are solution-seekers and will provide the solution or recommend another trusted company if we are not right for the job.

We are developing long-lasting relationships with our clients. I get to know them and always ask how things are going outside of the sale. I want all our customers to walk away feeling great after all interactions with our company while getting the information they need and being provided with great service.

Staying in touch and communicating is so important, even if it is over the phone. I listen to them and they know they have been heard. I love sales, the feeling that we are making a difference for our customers because of what we do and how we do it.

We want to do the job that we were hired for, but also do a bit extra that makes them say, "That was so great! I am really happy and will tell all my friends, thank you." Something that the customer will remember and think that that one small thing we did made their day. Our employees feel great about doing that, and they love seeing the customer's smile or hearing how awesome the job was done.

If we happen to get an abrupt or rude customer, our policy is to respect and treat them with kindness.

You can maintain a high level of service by knowing what is going on in the Company and among your employees. It's a matter of "feeling" intuition based on experience. I know what I must do to improve. I know what my job is, and my feelings will indicate whether I've done my job in the best way possible. This might have to do with a customer, a quotation, a phone call, or a discussion with an employee.

As an owner, I need to know that what I am doing feels great and what I've done is complete. When there's something that I've missed, something that I've run out of time to do, or someone I need to talk with, I get a nagging feeling that "pushes" me to finish what needs to be done.

I will proactively figure out the best way to handle the situation. I'm as proactive as possible so that our customers and our employees feel that they have all the information and the support they need from the Company.

There's got to be a flow between me and my business, from my business to my employees, and then from the employees to the customers. They all flow in synergy.

"Happy employees lead to happy customers which leads to more profits."

Vaugh Aust

Of course, the employees are always foremost in my mind. To encourage them, I listen to everything they say, and I do my best to make their work as easy as possible. I know it is not always easy because their jobs are physically demanding. I want their heads to be in the game, doing what they do, and not worrying about a problem or something that I did not complete. I'm proactive so I can ensure that each team feels supported. I'm always listening, encouraging and inspiring them, ensuring they have the equipment to do their job, ensuring they know their opinions matter, showing appreciation and recognition for a job well done.

Keeping Employees and Customers Happy

Being a small business owner can be lonely, even though you have all your employees surrounding you. They look up to you and you can't put your frustrations, uncertainties or business decisions on them. Your employees can not be part of your emotional support system, you can only be theirs.

My business partner and I bounce ideas off each other as well as support and cheerlead each other. We are both resourceful and have different strengths that enhance different parts of the business; when one person gets swamped the other is there to pick up where it is needed. We have each other's backs and we are the emotional support system for each other.

I need the following to run our company successfully:

1. Bring the best high-performance version of myself to work every day

2. Put structures in place so I can be and do my best

3. Support in areas that are not my expertise (accounting, tech stuff, safety coordinator etc.)

4. A sounding board – someone to brainstorm with who challenges me, has a sense of business and growth

5. A business coach - someone who believes in me and in what I am doing, who will call me out on my stuff and inspire my greatness

6. Time out to dream and be inspired about the business

7. A strong mission and vision that pulls me forward every day

8. Employees – effective communication, challenge them, engage them, support their ideas, acknowledge them and the skills they bring to the team

9. Communication with my customers

I'm here for one reason: to bring my best self to work every day so that our employees, our customers, and our company are successful. Bringing my best self happens through the power of my beliefs. Every day, I check in on my beliefs and listen to the beliefs of my employees and the overall company.

If I'm not bringing the best of me to work, then I need to change my perspective.

When my beliefs are aligned, I'm empowered which affects my business, things are flowing, but if they are not, then the power of my beliefs will feel challenging and this can also flow to my employees, which will affect the type of day that they are having and the experience our customers will have. This can become a big deal if it happens often enough.

My job is to bring my best to work. I have and follow a daily regime to stay on track and be my best with the right mindset. This keeps me on track and keeps me inspired for continual growth.

The Power of Your Beliefs

Your beliefs create the shape of your life including how you run your business. It is a daily game. You must believe in yourself and in your ability to run your company successfully.

When you are a business owner, it's very easy to get drawn into having negative beliefs that won't bring success to your company. Ensure that your beliefs will drive your company to be successful and inspiring for all. With our beliefs, we are either moving towards or away from something. If you are frustrated, you need a check in process, so you are aware of your current thoughts and if need be change your thoughts by following a daily regime to empowerment. We all have a familiar natural belief system that we fall back into out of habit whether or not it is good for us or our business.

"My beliefs are creating my reality."

Susan Delano Swim

Our beliefs, the key to our continual happiness and success, are based on our assumptions, expectations, and what stories we have created about a situation. Our beliefs have been with us from the beginning. Sometimes we challenge our beliefs because they no longer feel right, or you may never think to question your beliefs or realize that there is a process to help you change your thoughts/beliefs.

If you have owned an unsuccessful business, you may believe that you are not good at running a business. This is a belief based on a story that you created from an experience. If you don't address this belief, it will remain true because you said it was true, you now believe this to be your forever truth, "I am not good at being a boss or owning my own business."

You may be just scraping by financially, thinking that you are not a very good business owner. You are great at sales but not great at the other aspects of running your business. The problem with this belief is that you are not doing all that you can to be a successful business owner because you have set limitations by deciding it's difficult or that you are not good at it.

The truth is that all the experiences that we have, good or bad, experiencing riches or bankruptcy are an integral part of our growth and learning curve. Giving up would be a waste of this experience /education leaving you with a feeling that you cannot do it. Many of the most successful people in the world have experienced business failure or bankruptcy and have used those experiences to their advantage now knowing what not to do. Getting attached to the "I can't do, I am not good enough, I am not smart enough" will leave you feeling inept until you jump in and change your story, make something out of your experience, don't let that experience make something out of you.

Our beliefs create our reality, they are our foundation for how we do everything, what we can and cannot do, they are what we live by each moment of each day. Look at your beliefs and make sure they align with what you want in your personal life, your social life, and your business.

Our beliefs will bring us happiness or drive our happiness away. We are responsible for our beliefs, so choose ones that feel good, ones you can love that will support all aspects of your life.

To have a successful, well run business have the beliefs that will allow you to succeed!

"You can not have a happy ending to an unhappy journey."
Abraham Hicks

My decisions create the life I want. When we first started this company, my beliefs and actions were not going to get us the results that we needed or wanted. There were days when I was wishing but not problem-solving.

If you're wishing for a change, that becomes a problem. Wishing means you are not taking action; you are giving your powers up to a wish, hoping for the best. You must take action for any wished or desired change. Your beliefs and decisions must align with the Company in order to be powerful and successful. Check in with your beliefs so that your actions and decisions are the best for you and for your company.

If you're stuck in a wishful or negative thinking mode, then you'll make decisions that are not the best because your thoughts are disempowering which are very different from empowering thoughts. Empowering thoughts such as "This is a great company. I can do this. I am smart. I can make anything happen. I can create magic" will move you forward. Opposed to these disempowering thoughts "I can't do this, I don't care anymore, I am too stressed to think clearly" which will keep you having emotionally disabling thoughts confirming that you are not good at what you are doing.

Many years ago, I ran three businesses at one time, the construction company, I co-partnered in a property management company plus I was running and creating products in my coaching business. Being hands-on daily for each venture was definitely too much. I thought I was being smart; I started the property management company thinking that I would run my own show and have only a few employees to manage. What an eye-opener. As much as I loved our customers, I disliked my role. I heard nothing but complaints every day. I could do 20 things right but miss one email and I became a terrible person. The crazy thing is they liked me, but I still couldn't please everyone. The worst part was I couldn't do my other two jobs properly because the property management business consumed all my time.

After giving the property management business two years, I decided to sell my portion of the business. It was the best decision I ever made. I was no longer tied down to a computer screen. I could finally breathe again and recharge my creativity. What I did get from this business was a whole new appreciation for property managers, how many moving parts they have and how demanding and thankless their job is. I learned how to work better with property managers and make their jobs easier. If you can make your customers' life easier, they will love you and want to work with you.

I have also learned that having a daily routine helps keep my energy, productivity and confidence in check with all the moving pieces that I have at any given time. There are days where I'm in the middle of pure chaos and people ask, "How do you manage this, and manage it so well?"

I need to pull myself out of the chaos to take a breather and check on my beliefs before I return to it. I have daily routines and I have created tools that keep me on track. When I follow these structures and use my tools, I have fantastic days, no matter what is going on. Remember I told you I had the "Ass in Chair Syndrome" and that was debilitating for my creativity and inspiration. Now I get up and physically move from my desk on scheduled breaks. I get water, go for little walks, stretch, look out the window or do something to clear my mind; I take "brain breaks." When I come back to my desk, I bring freshness and new ideas, I feel uplifted so that my tasks get done quicker with my newfound creativity for the project. When you stop thinking about a problem that you just can't let go of, put some space between your thoughts and the problem, the solution shows up.

One day, I was running from my office to a friend's car. The day was full, busy as usual and I was really looking forward to getting away, even if just for a few hours. I was surprised when my friend said there was a calmness about me that she could feel. What I love about her comment is knowing what I do every day with my routines and practices is keeping me in that space. I don't feel anxiety or anxiousness over my workload because of how I work, everything that needs to be handled is, and I do feel that calmness. This wasn't something that I thought about until she mentioned it and I love that she could sense it.

Six daily steps I believe are required to be successful:

1. **First thing in the morning take 10 minutes to just be** and then I do this again when I first enter my office. Both at home before my day starts and, in the office, I clear my thoughts, get present, do 10 deep breaths, drink water, and set my intentions for the day. This simple step sets me up for a great day and removes any residual stress I might be carrying.

2. **Belief check ins** – to remain feeling inspired and make sure my decisions are powerful and good for the Company, our customers and our employees. I check in with my thoughts and my attitude. Make sure there are no disempowering negative beliefs that are sneaking in. I have conscious awareness to stay on track - one of the quickest ways of doing this is by thinking about the day ahead of me and paying attention to my feelings about it. Visualizing and stating my intentions of who and how I want to be for the day sets my day up on the right foot.

3. **The power behind energy rejuvenation several times daily**
   - I stretch and do breathing exercises every 60 minutes. I will also get up and walk around, have a snack, get a glass of water, and stop focused thinking to clear my thoughts which allows me to come back to my project at hand totally refreshed with new ideas.

4. **Self-confidence** – feeling happy and confident from the inside out, making sound decisions that feel right that benefit the Company. If my head is fighting my intuition questioning which way to go, I will always take the time, walk away and have the courage / confidence to follow my heart, to follow what feels better.

5. **Daily check in** – I ask myself everyday how I can do things better? Step back, walk away, how can I improve and then implement? I check in with my happiness level every day. If I am not happy or I am feeling stressed, or I feel too busy and anxious, I check in, I shift, I get present. Doing this will set me up to do better business, business of possibility, and I am happier doing what I must do.

6. **Daily Planner** – Every day before I start work, just after taking 10 minutes to just be, I fill in my daily planner sheet. This is all about staying on track and accomplishing what is important that day for our company. In the past, I would have tried to remember what I didn't want to forget to get done that day in order to have a great day. Nine times out of ten, I would go home with one important task not completed which never felt good. At the end of the book is a sample of the daily planner sheet that I use, or you can download it at: **www.susandelanoswim.com/daily**

Enjoy and embrace the journey every day: happiness at work - inspired, innovative, productive solutions seeking. The daily evolution of your business is your journey, it is where you spend your time, so you may as well enjoy it or why bother doing it.

When you own a business, you're on a journey. How you enjoy this journey is up to you. The business doesn't make it good or bad. It's who you are in the business and how you handle everything, how you show up and what you believe about your business, your customers, and your employees that makes the difference.

All the challenges we face, and I've had plenty - are part of what makes this journey so special. The challenges inspire innovation and push us to do business differently, helping us grow and develop.

"Never, never, never give up."

Winston Churchill

If you're aligned with your goals and are working towards achieving them, it's an awesome feeling of empowerment. You feel like you're doing exactly what you are meant to be doing. You know what works and what doesn't. You know what behaviors, beliefs, and attitudes help you; that's all within your control.

Know your beliefs and remind yourself of them every day. For example: I am an awesome high-performance leader for my company! I need that belief if I expect to be a high-performance leader in a high-performance company. That is my core belief that moves me forward each day.

"We must be the change we want to see in the world."

Mahatma Gandhi

This quote is true of our businesses as well. This statement encompasses connecting, communication, respect, transparency, value, appreciation, serving others, our employees and our customers. I live by this in my business. I am happy and inspired when all aspects are in alignment.

As much as my employees want to be inspired, so do I. I need to be motivated and pushed forward by what I do and how I do it. Feeling and showing my excitement is part of how we are inspiring our teams and clients. How I'm showing up and dealing with all aspects of our business puts everything in alignment.

We started our company with a goal of being able to retire when we felt the time was right. We would sell the Company for top dollar and then move on to the next phase. Over the years, I've added other aspects to that goal; I added details to that goal that were very fulfilling. Now, I also want to be recognized as leading edge experts in our area of expertise and have the proudest, happiest employees possible, ones who truly care about the Company. I set the intention every morning to have our company recognized as the high-performance leading-edge experts in our industry and strive to meet that goal every day.

Over Time, Your Goals and Needs Change

When we first started this company, I was not inspired. With all my efforts over the years, the Company was not growing as I felt it should, but neither had I. I hadn't found my passion or excitement for the company; it was just a job, I was just helping my husband out. I wanted to grow the business to be successful and profitable, so we could sell it, but had no direction or enthusiasm. I wasn't emotionally invested because I hadn't decided what I wanted or how I was going to be in the Company, and I wasn't inspired by what we were doing.

One day I looked in the mirror and took responsibility for our company's position and the lack of inspiration and success I felt. I was not in alignment or doing business to get us to our desired outcome which was necessary to have if I ever hoped to sell the business for top dollar.

The first step toward this was to develop a vision that would inspire me and allow me to become emotionally invested. My self-talk, daily actions and emotional exercises where developed. Raising the bar for me and the Company changed everything. Because we had made such great changes and were finding excellent employees, we became recognized as one of the best companies in this industry in Nova Scotia. Running the Company became easier every day. You can't do that unless you're emotionally invested. Everything must feel right. The first step is recognizing your need for something different when a situation calls for a change. For me looking inward is where I must go first. You must see that there is room for improvement.

Before, I would have said, "I needed work-life balance," sometimes you get so caught up in seeking that we make life harder than needed. Now, work-life balance is just part of what I do. I have good structures in place that creates a natural balance and making sure that everybody in the Company is set up for this as well will make their jobs feel better as well.

Part of my work-life balance has just become a flow. If you work too hard at trying to make something balance, it won't, because you're trying or pushing too hard creating resistance. Put some steps in place so that the balance starts to happen and evolve. If you don't start with the simple balance steps, finding balance may stay on your wish list, simplicity and stepping stones are key to embracing change.

When you are a small business owner you may get caught up in "I must do it all syndrome," which means long hours, exhaustion, frustration, no time for family or fun, or time to do what you love about the business (your vision). When you are operating at this belief system, your needs are not being met. I know this belief and I know it well.

At first, I didn't want to put extra resources into the Company especially since we could drive ourselves harder to do it, after all we were not making any money. This was a debilitating belief that I had created, which resulted in financial stagnation. I could not do what I love to do - customer relations, sales, and supporting our employees because I told myself I had to do everything else.

What finally changed is I became efficient by developing high-performance leadership habits and teams. For me to become a high-performance leader, I could only do what I was good at and had to find the support I needed for the remaining responsibilities.

It was such a relief and our business grew exponentially from this internal shift. There is no better feeling than knowing all your needs are being met.

Before, I envisioned, "Build it and sell it." My vision has changed over the years. My current vision is to be the best high-performance leader training experts in our industry. To be the best at what you want to do, it cannot be mechanical. You must bring your passion into what you're doing. Develop yourself and train your employees. If you are at your best and your employees are not, the company will be out of alignment and it will feel like a struggle.

If your employees don't share your company's vision of being leading edge experts, they will default to mediocre work. You must share your vision of having the best company with your employees. They will then have a goal, know what is expected of them and be proud of their work. With the right structure, your employees will understand exactly what you are seeking and will perform to meet your expectations and will set expectations of themselves.

I don't see anything going on with the Company as real problems anymore. I'm very proud of what we've achieved. I know as long as I am working from integrity, using my foundation of facts and knowledge from my business experience, paying attention to my feelings and setting my intentions for the desired outcomes; we are on the right track. If it feels right, it looks right, and people are great, then I know we are going in the right direction.

One of the inspired changes that my partner wanted to embrace was to come as close as possible to becoming a paperless company. We had the paper trail for everything we did, and I wasn't sure how this would work out. We decided to become as paperless as possible wherever we could. At first, I just couldn't envision going digital, although I knew this would potential save a lot of time and tracking. I had to trust that we could all make it work.

We're still 10% paper, but it has taken huge pressure off the Company in terms of payroll, estimates, work orders, hazard assessments, getting jobs signed off and then collecting, tracking and filing all of it. We are now digital. The office now has immediate real-time access to everything. We are no longer wasting time searching for their paperwork or hearing they did it but can't find it or coffee spilled on it. It saves us a lot time and hassle. It has been well worth the trial and errors of setting it up and has proven to be very effective and efficient.

The Excitement and Inspiration Will Drive the Growth

Our company's vision comes from feeling inspired and setting intentions for myself and the Company. There's always room for growth, no matter what I am doing.

I am driven by sales and love the "thrill of the chase and the win."

Winning a project bid with a new client who typically used our competition and then getting to show how great our company is, is a thrill for me, it is my excitement and inspiration to keep driving forward.

If you're not feeling inspired, you are probably stuck in status quo, which is a place of automation: following the same old steps and routines hoping for at least the same results if not a little bit better. It is definitely not inspiring or high performance and over time your company will start to show signs of falling behind.

I'm always looking to push the Company to the next level. Inspiration and excitement keep you motivated. When I don't feel inspired, then I must envision what will be the next best step for the company.

There is a catch with always looking for growth. When you focus too much on growth, it can become a constant chase of "not enough." I make sure that I show gratitude for every employee and customer, I have gratitude and appreciation for what the Company gives me and my family. When I come from this place looking for what is next, it is fun and exciting. I'm very fortunate to have a group of employees who want to grow with the Company and do their best. They constantly give me ideas about how they can improve what they're doing so that the Company can grow.

For instance, our supervisor, gets asked quite frequently to do jobs on the side. How can he handle this situation differently so that people don't walk away when he says, "No, I'll have to go through the Company"! He talked to me to devise a plan, "How can we pull these people in as customers, break the illusion that it's too expensive, and what can he do when he's talking to those that approach him?" We devised a plan.

Some employees might not even tell their bosses that this is happening. Some might just go do the work. We had this happen. An old supervisor did a job and asked his team members to participate. Because he was the supervisor they thought they were doing the job for the Company and realized after doing the same job a couple of times that the supervisor was putting the cash in his pocket. The team members came to me immediately because they did not want anything to do with it. This supervisor was let go and the team was rebuilt.

Had this not happened, the team would've completely fallen apart just watching this one employee abuse his position. Inspire your employees to talk with you and do their best work and follow through when you are brought situations/problems. Sometimes stuff happens but building trust and respect with your employees will help solve the problem.

As an employer you must trust that everything is being done well and that your employees are representing the Company the best that they can. Micromanaging is a sign that you don't feel confident in their ability. When I did this, I got a feeling of not being able to let go, of having to try to control from afar. Notice this and ensure your teams have all the training and information that they need so you don't get caught doing this unnecessary work.

I like to hope that I come from a vision of the greater good, I feel I do. Everything I do, I base on what is needed in the moment that will be part of our vision, what is happening with my employees and customers, what is best for our company. I pay attention to my feelings and intentions, and I pay attention to all this every day. They're my greatest guiding point. I can tell when I'm talking to my employees how in alignment we are in that moment for that day.

I'm fortunate to have what we consider the best employees in the industry, doing exceptional work. Know what motivates your teams, so that you can use that motivation in your work plan.

We all have moments when we are not attuned to our feelings. Always pay attention to them because they are your signal something's great or not quite right. When feeling uneasy about something that you have not dealt with, such as talking to an employee about a situation or something that happened, your emotions are letting you know you must take action. They will keep bugging you until you've resolved it. It doesn't go away because we wish it away or have pushed it to the back of your thoughts.

You will feel excited and happy, an internal high when you are progressing towards your vision and representing your mission statement. Acknowledge this progress, be proud of yourself, celebrate and share it with your team.

Everything Always Comes Back to Communication

Communication is the key to everything: my customers, employees, business partner, and office staff. Communication is vital. I also believe in recognition for the work that our employees have accomplished and how they represent our company.

There's nothing easy about what we do. Our teams work hard every day and I feel they need to know that I recognize and appreciate their efforts; I have a job because they do their job. Without my employees, I could go get all the work in the world and if no one was there to do it and especially do it well to keep our customers happy, then I wouldn't have a company.

Trust that good decisions are being made by everyone from the top down. It is achieved easier by the processes that you have in place to create an environment in which trust will grow:

1. **Communication** – honest communication and active listening is critical, lack of communication may make your employees feel unimportant and will lead to a feeling of not being valued in your company

2. **Trust factor** – do what you say you will do, stand by your employees, always have their back, always communicate any changes

3. **Employee training** – know what trainings and strengths

an employee has so you can position them in the absolute best job for their abilities and interests. Know what future trainings interest them and devise a plan.

4. **Meet on common ground** – get to know each other, know what they are capable of professionally, and get to know what is important to them personally. Share the companies vision and your personal values, your work ethic, let them know how you work and what you like about how they work

5. **Job security** – if you value your employees let them know, they want to hear it. If you are having trouble with an employee, let them know, they may want the opportunity to improve what is not working well before it is too late

I trust that everybody's doing exactly what they should be doing. If an employee gives you a reason to distrust them, that's something you need to handle. Don't keep living with it; don't allow it to filter through your team so that you now have a huge problem with everybody on your team. Your employees will know whether you trust them just by how you handle things and what you say.

When we appreciate the Company, we receive so many gifts.

My employees give me the **gift of peace**. Peace that everything is going as it should go and that we have each other's back. I'm open with my employees. I've always made them feel that they can come to me with anything. If there's a way that we can support them, we will support them personally and professionally.

I also get the **gift of pride**. I've heard my employees and supervisors say how proud they are of their team because they're having fun, working hard, and everyone is going above and beyond to provide excellent service to our customers. The pride they take in their daily work is peace of mind for me.

The **gift of great leadership**. Coming from the top down to lead your groups so your team leaders have the confidence and ability to guide their crews.

The **gift of confidence**. Proper training and communication means your teams feel great and both they and I have the confidence in their performance.

It all falls together. Everybody knows what they're doing and gets their work done. They're all supporting each other and the Company. They report how their day went, I support them, and their decisions and we start all over the next day.

Nothing major has happened for years now, because they all know what they're doing and where they're going.

We have had the odd negative employee. They don't last long because they diminish the Company's flow and they are hard to be around. You will notice a decline, a difference in your team's morale and in the amount of work that's getting done, and the only thing that's changed is a negative person has joined the team.

Everybody knows where they fit. They belong on this supportive team that continues bonding, growing, and fulfilling this vision.

All my guys have a plan of where they want to be within the Company in the next couple of years. They see themselves continuing to grow, and they make me part of that plan, which means they're not in status quo, they are not settling. They're inspired to do more, do better, and further themselves within the Company. They've also picked their replacements. They're training them to do their jobs so they themselves can progress.

There's a constant unfolding of new abilities and motivations, and there's a community spirit within our teams. It makes the growth and evolution of the Company effortless.

When we first got involved in this company and we had all these employees that came from the past owner, it was a disaster.

It took us sometime to figure out that the disaster had nothing to do with the employees. It had everything to do with our expectations, how we were currently running the Company, how that past company was run and what they were used to.

One day, I had this moment in the mirror: "It's not the employees that are the problem. It's me, it's us. We need to step up as leaders."

As soon as we assumed responsibility for what was going on in the Company, the shift began within the employees. There was much more communication and sifting through who would and wouldn't be part of our team. There was an awakening and some fear when we looked at our employees realizing none of the employees where fitting the bill, fitting the vision of the company, but if you let them all go, who would do all the work.

I know as a business owner; we get very comfortable with the staff that we know. The old saying is, "At least you know the devil you're working with." But if you feel that way, that they are the devil, you're not treating them as a true team member. To have the team that you want, you must feel inspired by whom you're working with and that you're all giving your best.

To sum up...

Staying present is key to doing and being your best. Create a big vision with a mission statement for your company and keep your eye on the prize - your vision. Whatever your vision is, keep it close. My vision is to build a successful company that is the best in Halifax and is leading edge in the industry with respected high-performance technicians working in teams, that are self-driven, inspired by what is possible and support the Company to the best of their ability.

I visualize through meditation how I want my life and our journey to be. I get inspired by the path that we are on: we are staying on track working towards our vision as it evolves every year. I revisit my vision and make it grow as I grow.

As our company's sales increased and its reputation grew, everything became easier. We were winning great tenders/contracts and work was getting done efficiently. Our sales were coming from high profile clients, we became known as the "go-to" company with the best workers in town. We were exceeding our sales targets every month and our employees were out performing all their past jobs. Magic was happening, I was having fun, and I was extremely proud of what we had accomplished. My biggest vision was our new reality and my vision for the Company is now even bigger.

Believing in possibility, staying positive and happy with my six daily routines are a big part of keeping me on track.

Don't wait to be happy. I got caught in the early years of growing our company. I kept saying, when we get to this point I can breathe, I can relax, but until then I'm in the bump and grind. I didn't realize that I was postponing my happiness and I wasn't appreciating the steps, the process, the learning curve, and the journey that it took to get where we were going. It is never good to postpone your happiness or being in the present moment, always putting that off could become a habit for you. When you are happy in the present moment you will always do better work, you will always be positive, you will always be more creative, you will always be a better boss, spouse and parent. It is never a good idea to postpone happiness and it is never a good idea to not appreciate what you have, i.e.: I will be happy when we show a profit. It will take you twice as long and it will feel painfully exhausting to get to where you are going. Plus, you will miss all the good stuff that is in the process of getting there. You are just making life harder than it has to be. Have the right mindset to grow your business and you will enjoy the journey, no matter what stage you are in.

Happiness is a choice! If you are someone who needs to learn to generate happy feelings, to practice/work your happiness muscle, there are exercises that you can do every day to help you be happier with everything you have to do.

In this chapter we have talked about what I do and check in on a daily basis to stay on track and to stay excited with a big vision for our company. It is easy to just go to work and work your business but that is not necessarily the best way to run your business.

A quick summarization:

- Importance of Intuition, feeling good to improve
- Company Synergy - leaders to employees to customers
- 9 Attributes to running our company
- The importance of your belief system
- My business path
- Daily check in to stay on path
- 6 daily steps to success
- The journey
- Setting daily intentions
- Aligning your vision with your growth
- Leading company on my guiding points, feelings and setting intentions
- Have a Big Vision for your company
- Power behind your Mission Statement
- Creating a trusting environment
- 5 Gifts
- Enjoy the journey, be happy now and believe anything is possible

It is important to schedule times to consistently work on your business in the role of a visionary. Most business owner become entrenched working in the daily operations of their business and forget to work on their business. Your vision for the company, the growth on the horizon, is the success path of your company and a big piece of the excitement that will keep you, your employees and clients attracted to your company. Creating possibility and stretching beyond your comfort zone is how you started your company so don't stop doing that part because you are comfortable, discouraged or just too stressed out running everything. Create possibility and become the inspired leader that you where when you where dreaming about your company. Become the high-performance leader that will take your company to the next level, in the end it is up to you where you and your company go!

CONCLUSION

Help through High Performance Leadership Training

WHY WILL COACHING WITH me transform your world? We all swing between being motivated and being unmotivated. We have days with high ambitions - a mission, goals and a drive to accomplish great things We feel alive, connected and creative. Then there are days when you feel lost, confused, disappointed, unclear and frustrated. This is the life of an entrepreneur/business owner!

Being a business owner can be exhausting. You are on 100% of the time even when you are trying to take time off. You are performing tasks in your company that are not your expertise just to get them done. You are overwhelmed most days with the ins and outs of running your business. You are constantly being derailed, pulled in multiple directions or putting fires out. You are not doing the role you dreamed of - what you love. You don't have time to even think about that role let alone fill the role of being an inspired leader working on your business vision because you are consumed by the daily mechanics of operating your business.

You know you are smart and have what it takes to be success-ful. You have gotten yourself to where you are today, but you also know in your heart there is more for you, another level of success. You know all this but don't know how you can possibly deal with one more thing. Your energy is already tapped out and your productivity isn't what you want it to be.

This is when you hire an expert who has specific skills for clarity, productivity, a new level of focus and confidence. One who can understand your stressors and knows what the next best moves are for you in your business. An expert will help you break through to find that level of clarity, to feel confident making decisions, to rejuvenate your energy and to be more productive so you are able to say with confidence: "This is who I am, this is what I want, this is where I am growing next".

This is what my program offers my clients, that is why it is so powerful. When I took ownership of where I was in the business and my responsibilities, my world changed. How I did everything changed. This program was my change!

Working with me will help challenge you to rise to your best self and to think bigger while being congruent with who you are and your values; keep you on track; set up high performance leadership routines; direct you towards accelerated growth with guidance to rise above the noise, distractions and negativity. Become excited by your business again, bring joy to the process AND to learn how to be a stress-free leader.

Being an entrepreneur can be lonely. Having me on your side every week to increase your energy, clarity and confidence, to keep you moving forward, is priceless. There is a structure to becoming a high-performance leader, it doesn't happen on its own. Every session has an outcome that will move you forward no matter what it is you do. That's the power of having a confidante, a coach that is highly skilled to ask the right questions, and who has the right process for you to continue your growth in all areas of your life and only has your best interest in mind. To become a true high-performance leader, to achieve top levels of success in your life, you need a plan. A plan that will lift your life in a holistic way to have a sustained ability to be in a flow, to feel joy, and to achieve yours dreams at this time in your life.

Components of High-Performance Leadership Training

1. Creating new sustainable habits that will help you excel in your leadership role knowing there is a better way to do business

2. How having the right habits will create more success in your business and in your life, struggle shouldn't be part of your business norm or expectation.

3. Learn to love figuring out challenges, they are not to be ignored or feared. They are your growth moments.

4. Gain knowledge on your responsibility, the parts you play in your business for its success or lack of it

5. High-Performance Leadership Training 12-week program that will deliver new habit-forming tools and insights that will rock who you are and how you lead your business

Teaching business owners how to stay inspired in their business when times get tough is a passion of mine. My many different business experiences have taught me numerous hands on strategies while continuing my education in this arena since 1999 providing me with many tools to focus on leadership development, employee retention, attraction and engagement along with team building initiatives. My broad experience base includes being creative to find solutions and inspiration for all the different dynamics that happen when you are the owner / operator of your business and have the desire / need to be inspiring to your staff so they can be the best that they can be. I will work with you either privately or in a group setting teaching this training.

If this sounds like you, if you are looking for more, I invite you to fill out an application and schedule your complimentary call at www.susandelanoswim.com/application

Always, wishing you the best,

Susan

Susan's Information

Contact – Susan@susandelanoswim.com

Let's Chat:

Application Form – www.susandelanoswim.com/application

Downloads

Daily Planner Sheet – www.susandelanoswim.com/daily

High-Performance Leadership Exercises – www.susandelanoswim.com/exercises

facebook.com/susandelanoswim

instagram.com/susandelanoswim

https://twitter.com/SusanDSwim

https://ca.linkedin.com/in/susandswim

Daily Planner

Date _____

Waking Moments: Did I prepare myself for the best day possible at home and the office?	Yes	No

Daily Projects: The 3 *most* important things I **must** do today to move my business forward?

1. _____
2. _____
3. _____

Top 3 Priorities I Must Get Done	Who I Must Talk To:
1.	1.
2.	2.
3.	3.

Passion Project - set a time along with your next best steps

Daily Reminders:

Water	1	2	3	4

Brain Breaks: Every 50 to 60 minutes took 5-10 minute break	Yes	No
Gratitude and Appreciation - did I reflect today and practice	Yes	No

Intentions

Did I practice my personal intentions (3 words)	Yes	No
Did I practice my interaction intentions when I needed to (3 words)	Yes	No

Rate Self (rate 1 to 10) Was I a great leader today?	Rate ____	Yes	No

One thing I can do now to be a better leader

Tomorrow I will

www.ingramcontent.com/pod-product-compliance
Lightning Source LLC
Chambersburg PA
CBHW071155200326
41519CB00018B/5231